THE FIVE

I0155543

SOLAS:

AN EXPOSITORY

EXHORTATION

NATHAN W. TUCKER

1689
Reformed Baptist Press

ISBN: 979-8-218-57693-6

1689
Reformed Baptist Press

NATHAN W. TUCKER

Dedicated to my beloved wifey, Lisa, my perfect jigsaw puzzle piece! Without your love, support, encouragement, and wisdom, this book would never have happened.

The author wishes to express his heartfelt gratitude to all those who have taken of their valuable time to edit this material and offer suggestions to make this book better. All errors and mistakes in this book are my own. The author would be indebted to any reader who, so desiring, wishes to send corrections to him at reformedbaptistpress@gmail.com.

NATHAN W. TUCKER

TABLE OF CONTENTS

PREFACE

This book is adapted from a sermon series I gave on the *Five Solas* of the Protestant Reformation: that salvation—found in Scripture alone—is through grace alone, by faith alone, in Christ alone, to the glory of God alone. While these *Solas* originally developed as a protest against the apostate Roman Catholic Church in the 16th century, their importance is no less vital 500 years later in a post-modern, post-Christian 21st century.

The sufficiency, inerrancy, and infallibility of Scripture remain under constant attack on all fronts. The deity of Christ, the sufficiency of His blood, and the exclusivity of His atonement are continually blasphemed by moral relativism. Far too many professing believers have eviscerated *Sola Fide* by replacing it with mere head knowledge + good works. And far too many genuine believers have not been taught that the only salvation that can possibly be by grace alone for God's glory alone is one that is monergistic rather than semi-Pelagian synergism.

This book, therefore, is an expositional explanation of the *Five Solas* to exhort the Church to "contend earnestly for the faith once for all delivered to the saints" (Jude 3). These *Solas*, first elucidated in Scripture, expounded by Augustine and the other Church Fathers, and then revived by the Reformers, is the creed upon which the Church must stand or it has not only failed Christ in the world, but denied Christ to the world. This is our hope, or we have no hope. This is our witness, or we have no witness. O Lord, may we hold fast the confession of our hope without wavering (Heb. 10:23)!

Nathan W. Tucker
Christmas 2024

1 SOLA SCRIPTURA

We will begin our study with *Sola Scriptura*—the principle that the means of salvation is only revealed in Scripture alone. The very first lie recorded in Scripture is found in Genesis 3:1, in which Satan tempted Eve in the Garden of Eden, asking, "'Did God really say...?'" (NIV84). And that lie is the lie that the Church has had to combat every since —"Did God really say...?'" This is the lie of cults and heresies, false religions and post-modern culture—"'Did God really say...?'" The fight for *Sola Scriptura*, therefore, is fundamental to the Christian faith. It is fundamental to our understanding of the Triune God, truth & reality, and the redemption brought by the Incarnate God. Upon it hang all the other Reformation *Solas* of grace alone, through faith alone, in Christ alone, to the glory of God alone. Without it, there is no Christianity. This is why the first and longest chapter of the Second London Baptist Confession of Faith (1689) is entirely about *Sola Scriptura*.

There are six foundational and essential components encompassed in the phrase *Sola Scriptura*.

1. Inspiration.

The first and most fundamental component of *Sola Scriptura* is the inspiration of Scripture. All Scripture is divinely inspired, or breathed-out, by God. We see this unequivocally established in 2 Timothy, chapter 3, beginning with verse 16:

> 16 All Scripture is given by inspiration of God, and is profitable for doctrine, for reproof, for correction, for instruction in righteousness, 17 that the man of God

> may be complete, thoroughly equipped
> for every good work.
>
> (2 Tim. 3:16-17)

The first thing to note about verse 16 is the word *all*. It is the Greek word *pas*, which means all, every, the whole, every kind of. The second thing to note about verse 16 is that the Greek word translated as *Scripture* is *graphe*, which generically may simply mean *writing*. However, *graphe* is used 51 times in the New Testament, and every single time it is always, without fail, referring to Holy Scriptures. And the third and final thing to note from verse 16 is that the Greek word translated as *inspired* is *theopneustos*. The first part of *theopneustos* is *Theo*, which means God. The second part of *theopneustos* comes from the Greek word *pneo*, which means to blow or exhale. Put the two halves of the word together and *theopneuestos* literally means "breathed out by God."

In verse 16, therefore, the Apostle Paul is telling us that all Scripture is God-exhaled. Every single jot and tittle (Matt. 5:18) of the Bible has God as its author. This is what is meant by the phrase *the plenary and verbal inspiration of the Bible*. *Plenary* refers to all 66 books of the Old and New Testaments as being God-exhaled, whereas *verbal* means that every single word, as well as its verb tense and sentence placement in the original language, was divinely inspired. The entirety of Scripture —including all of its words and even its very grammar and syntax—where breathed out by God Himself.

By *inspiration*, therefore, we do not mean that God inspired men to write the Bible in the same way that we may describe a composer or artist as being inspired craftsmen. Rather, by the term *inspiration* we mean that it is God Himself speaking through human actors. However, this, in turn, does not mean that the human authors of Scripture were so completely controlled by God when they wrote the Biblical text so as to erase all differences in personality and character. *God-exhaled* simply means that God superintended the work of human authors. They were not mechanical mystics whose quills channeled the Holy Spirit as they flew across the page. Neither were they merely acting as secretaries taking down dictation from God as they wrote the Holy Scriptures. All of Scripture and everything contained in Scripture are the very words of God Himself, but superintended through the agency of human actors in a mysterious way that we cannot explain but only see ample proof of on every page of the Bible.

We read in 2 Peter, chapter 1:

> 19 And so we have the prophetic word confirmed, which you do well to heed as a light that shines in a dark place, until the day dawns and the morning star rises in your hearts; 20 knowing this first, that no prophecy of Scripture is of any private interpretation, 21 for prophecy never came by the will of man, but holy men of God spoke as they were moved by the Holy Spirit.
>
> (2 Pet. 1:19-21)

The Greek word for *interpretation* in verse 20 is *epilusis*, which literally means *unloosing* or *to release*. A form of the word, *epilyo*, is used throughout the New Testament to mean *unraveling*, *unpacking*, *expounding*, or *solving*. In other words, reading it in context of both verses 20 and 21, *epilusis* means that the authors of Scripture were not making it up out of their own imaginations, but rather as they were "moved by the Holy Spirit." The Greek word translated in verse 21 as *moved* is *phero*, which literally means *carried* or *borne*, which further confirms the mode of divine inspiration that we just discussed—namely, that the human authors of Scripture were carried (NIV84, ESV, ISV, NET) or borne (YLT) by the Holy Spirit as they wrote rather than dictated to as robotic machines.

Let's look at a few other places in Scripture where it authenticates itself to be the very word of God. The book of Hebrews begins by declaring:

> [1] God, who at various times and in various ways spoke in time past to the fathers by the prophets, [2] has in these last days spoken to us by His Son, whom He has appointed heir of all things, through whom also He made the world.
> (Heb. 1:1-2)

God spoke. God has not left Himself without a witness, but has sovereignly and graciously revealed Himself and HIs will to us in a book. He has not hidden Himself from us or left us guessing as to how we might please Him. No, He spoke through the Old Testament in which He gave promise after promise and prophecy after prophecy of what He was about to do, and then He spoke to us through the New Testament in which He confirms and fulfills the Old. In the Old testament God spoke through prophets; in the New He speaks through God the Son Jesus Christ and those whom the Son deputized (Jn. 14:25-26, 16:12) to complete the canon of Scripture.

For instance, in John 6:63, Jesus refers to His words as spirit and life, and a few verses later (vs. 68) Peter and the other apostles refuse to leave Him because, "You have the words of eternal life." We find in John, chapter 17,

Jesus' praying His High Priestly Prayer the night before His death:

> [6] "I have manifested Your name to the men whom You have given Me out of the world. They were Yours, You gave them to Me, and *they have kept Your word.* [7] Now they have known that all things which You have given Me are from You. [8] *For I have given to them the words which You have given Me*; and they have received them, and have known surely that I came forth from You; and they have believed that You sent Me...
>
> [13] But now I come to You, and these things I speak in the world, that they may have My joy fulfilled in themselves. [14] *I have given them Your word*; and the world has hated them because they are not of the world, just as I am not of the world. [15] I do not pray that You should take them out of the world, but that You should keep them from the evil one. [16] They are not of the world, just as I am not of the world. [17] Sanctify them by Your truth. Your word is truth."
>
> (Jn. 17:6-8, 13-17; emphasis added)

There are many, many things that could be said about this passage, but here we will focus on the following:

- **Verse 6:** "'...they have kept Your word.'"
- **Verse 8:** "'For I have given to them the words which You have given Me.'"
- **Verse 13:** "'...these things I speak in the world, that they may have My joy fulfilled in themselves."

• **Verse 14:** "I have given them Your word..."

In sum, therefore, we see that God spoke through the prophets in the Old Testament and through His Son in the New Testament.

Space will permit us to only reference a few other verses that authenticate the entirety of Scripture as God-exhaled. In Matthew 4:4, Jesus refers to it as the very words that proceed from the mouth of God. In Romans 3:2, the Apostle Paul refers to Scripture as the oracles of God. And in numerous places the New Testament authors refer to all of Holy Writ as the "Word of God."

In fact, in over 3,800 times in the Old Testament we find the words, "Thus says Yahweh," "The word of Yahweh came," or "God said." For instance, Isaiah begins his book with these words:

> 2 Hear, O heavens, and give ear, O earth!
> For Yahweh has spoken...
> 11 ...Says Yahweh...
> 18 ...Says Yahweh...
> 20 ...For the mouth of Yahweh has spoken...
> 24 Therefore—the affirmation of Adonai—
> Yahweh Sabaoth, the Mighty One of Israel...
> (Is. 1:2, 11, 18, 20, 24 NYLT)

Similarly, Jeremiah the prophet begins his book with these words: "unto whom the word of Yahweh has been" (Jer. 1:2 NYLT). And the author of 2 Chronicles states that Jeremiah was, "speaking from the mouth of Yahweh" (2 Chron. 36:12 NYLT; see also Ezra 1:1). In Exodus, God told Moses that, "I will be your mouth and teach you what you shall say" (4:12). In Galatians, the Apostle Paul writes:

> [11] But I make known to you, brethren, that the gospel which was preached by me is not according to man. [12] For I neither received it from man, nor was I taught it, but it came through the revelation of Jesus Christ.
>
> (Gal. 1:11-12; see also Acts 26:16; 1 Cor. 11:23)

In 1 Timothy, Paul quotes two other verses (Deut. 25:4 & Luke 10:7) and calls them both—one from the Old Testament and one from the New—as "Scripture" (5:18). In 2 Peter, the Apostle Peter calls Paul's epistles "Scripture" (3:15-16). Jude 17-18 quotes Peter (2 Peter 3:2) as Scripture. Finally, over and over again in Revelation, chapters 2 and 3, the Apostle John writes, "the Spirit says to the churches."

In short, Scripture is replete with self-authenticating statements that it is the very word of God. The entirety of Scripture—including all of its words and even its very grammar and syntax—where breathed out by God Himself. When the Bible speaks, God speaks. Therefore, to reject any part of Scripture is to reject God Himself, because it is His word.

2. Infallible.

The second component of *Sola Scriptura* is the infallibility of Scripture. *Infallibility* means that it is impossible for the Bible to contain any error or fault in all that it teaches. Because Scripture is the very words of God, they are as perfect as God Himself is perfect. For instance, Psalm 18:30 reads, "God!—perfect is His way! The saying of Yahweh is tried, a shield is He to all those trusting in Him!" (NYLT; see also 2 Sam. 22:31). Or Psalm

7

12:6, which proclaims, "The sayings of Yahweh are pure sayings, like silver tried in a furnace of earth, refined sevenfold" (NYLT). Or Psalm 119:140, which declares, "Your promises is well tried, and your servant loves it" (ESV).

We read in Psalm 19:

> 7 The law of Yahweh is perfect, refreshing the soul;
> The testimonies of Yahweh are steadfast, making wise the simple;
> 8 The precepts of Yahweh are upright, rejoicing the heart;
> The command of Yahweh is pure, enlightening the eyes;
> 9 The fear of Yahweh is clean, standing to the age;
> The judgments of Yahweh are true, they have been righteous—together.
> 10 They are more desirable than gold,
> Yea, than much fine gold;
> And sweeter also than honey, even liquid honey of the comb.
> 11 Also—Your servant is warned by them,
> In keeping them there is a great reward.
>
> (Ps. 19:7-11 NYLT)

Finally, Proverbs 30:5 proclaims that, "every word of God is flawless" (NIV84). Therefore, since God is perfect, all of His words must be perfect as well, and consequently it impossible for Scripture to contain any error or fault in all it teaches—no less in what it states about God's acts in creation, about the events of world history, and about its own literary origins under God, than in its witness to God's saving grace in individual lives. Or, to put it another way, if God's Word is fallible, then God must be as well, which means that He cannot, by very definition, be God after all.

3. Inerrant.

The third component of *Sola Scriptura* is the inerrancy of Scripture. Notice how these components of *Sola Scriptura* build upon each other—(1) the Bible is the very word of God; which of necessity means (2) that the Bible cannot error; which in turn now (3) must mean that the Bible contains no errors. That's what the word *inerrancy* means—that it has no mistakes or, to put it another way, that it does not lie. That it is absolute Truth without error or blemish.

Titus 1:2 declares that God cannot lie (see also Num. 23:19; 1 Sam. 15:29; Heb. 6:18), and in numerous other places it declares that an essential component or attribute of God is His truthfulness (Ex. 34:6; Deut. 32:4; Ps. 31:5, 57:10, 108:4; Is. 65:16; Jn. 14:6). And because God is Truth personified, Daniel 4:36 proclaims that all of His "works are truth." Not only that, but because God is Truth personified, the Bible is adamant that, as Jesus prayed in John 17:17, God's "word is truth."

Psalm 119:160 declares that, "[t]he entirety of Your word is truth" (Ps. 119:160), and in 2 Samuel 7:28 King David of Israel proclaimed, "And now, O Adonai Yahweh, You are God, and Your words are true..." (NYLT). Psalm 119:151 affirms that, "All [His] commands are true," and Hebrews 10:23 tells us that all of His promises can be trusted because "He who promised is faithful" (see also Heb. 6:13).

In short, Scripture is the inerrant Truth of God and therefore doesn't contain a single shred of error,

9

contradiction, deceit, fraud, or delusion within its pages. The Bible is indeceivable.

4. **Immutable.**

The fourth component of *Sola Scriptura* is the immutability of Scripture. We saw first that Scripture is divinely inspired by God. Secondly, that it is infallible or incapable of error. Third, that it is inerrant or truthful, incapable of deceit. Now, fourth, we see that the Bible is immutable or incapable of changing or failing over time. Because God is and always has been perfect, He is incapable—from eternity past to eternity future—of becoming more or less perfect. He is, consequently, immutable or unchangeable. And because God is immutable and unchangeable, His word must be as well.

In 1 Peter, chapter 1, we read:

> 22 Since you have purified your souls in obeying the truth through the Spirit in sincere love of the brethren, love one another fervently with a pure heart, 23 having been born again, not of corruptible seed but incorruptible, through the word of God which lives and abides forever, 24 because
> "All flesh is as grass,
> And all the glory of man as the flower of the grass.
> The grass withers,
> And its flower falls away,
> 25 But the word of the LORD endures forever."
> Now this is the word which by the gospel was preached to you.
>
> (1 Pet. 1:22-25)

Here Peter cites the Old Testament (Isaiah 40:6-8) to prove that the Gospel is the Word of Yahweh and therefore it lives and abides forever. In John 10:35, Jesus states that the Word of God "cannot be broken." In His Sermon on the Mount in Matthew 5, Jesus tells His disciples:

> [17] "Do not think that I came to destroy the Law or the Prophets. I did not come to destroy but to fulfill. [18] For assuredly, I say to you, till heaven and earth pass away, one jot or one tittle will by no means pass from the law till all is fulfilled.
>
> (Matt. 5:17-18)

And, again, in Matthew 24:35 Jesus declares that, "Heaven and earth will pass away, but My words will by no means pass away." Psalm 119:89 proclaims, "To the age, O Yahweh, Your word is set up in the heavens" (NYLT), and a few verses later, in 160, "and every one of Your righteous judgments endures forever." Consequently, just as God is immutable and unchangeable, so His word is immutable and unchangeable as well.

5. **Sufficient.**

The fifth component of *Sola Scriptura* is the sufficiency of Scripture. The Bible is entirely and completely sufficient to give the knowledge of God and His will which is necessary for salvation.

In Joshua, chapter 1, we find Yahweh telling Joshua after the death of Moses:

> [7] "Only be strong and very courageous, that you may observe to do according to all the law which Moses My servant commanded you; do

11

not turn from it to the right hand or to the left, that you may prosper wherever you go. 8 This Book of the Law shall not depart from your mouth, but you shall meditate in it day and night, that you may observe to do according to all that is written in it. For then you will make your way prosperous, and then you will have good success."

(Josh. 1:7-8)

God is telling Joshua that everything he needs to know about God's will in order to please Him is contained within Holy Writ. Again, in Isaiah, chapter 8, we are told:

19 And when they say to you, "Seek those who are mediums and wizards, who whisper and mutter," should not a people seek their God? Should they seek the dead on behalf of the living? 20 To the law and to the testimony! If they do not speak according to this word, it is because there is no light in them.

(Is. 8:19-20)

There is no need for any other revelation because everything necessary for God's glory and man's salvation is contained within Holy Writ. In Luke, chapter 16, we find Jesus telling a parable in which a rich man in hell is talking with Abraham in heaven:

27 "Then [the rich man] said, 'I beg you therefore, father [Abraham], that you would send [Lazarus] to my father's house, 28 for I have five brothers, that he may testify to them, lest they also come to this place of torment.'

> [29] Abraham said to him, 'They have Moses and the prophets; let them hear them.' [30] And he said, 'No, father Abraham; but if one goes to them from the dead, they will repent.' [31] But he said to him, 'If they do not hear Moses and the prophets, neither will they be persuaded though one rise from the dead.'"
>
> (Lk. 16:27-31)

Here Jesus is saying that there is no need for the testimony of a dead man raised to life because all that is necessary for God's glory and man's salvation is contained within Holy Writ (see also 2 Thess. 2:2). Finally, returning to 2 Timothy, chapter 3, we read:

> [16] All Scripture is given by inspiration of God, and is profitable for doctrine, for reproof, for correction, for instruction in righteousness, [17] that the man of God may be complete, thoroughly equipped for every good work.
>
> (2 Tim. 3:16-17)

No other revelation is needed, Paul says, because Holy Writ is absolutely and entirely sufficient in and of itself for a believer to be completely and thoroughly prepared for every good work. Therefore, either expressly set down in the pages of Scripture or necessarily contained therein is the whole counsel of God concerning all things necessary for His own glory, man's salvation, faith, and life.

6. Final and complete.

The sixth and final component of *Sola Scriptura* is the finality and completeness of Scripture. Not only is the canon of Scripture so sufficient that no new or extra-

Biblical revelations are needed, but it is final and complete to the exclusion of new or extra-Biblical revelations.

In Deuteronomy, chapter 4, we find Moses commanding the Israelites:

> 1 `And now, Israel, give heed unto the statutes, and unto the judgments which I am teaching you to do, so that you live, and have gone in, and possessed the land which Yahweh God of your fathers is giving to you. 2 You do not add to the word which I am commanding you, nor diminish from it, to keep the commands of Yahweh your God which I am commanding you.
>
> (Deut. 4:1-2 NYLT)

In verse 1 Moses is reminding them that Scripture is sufficient for knowing God's will and pleasing Him, and in verse 2 he therefore warns them that it is complete and final and must not be added to or subtracted from. A few chapters over in Deuteronomy, chapter 12, we read:

> 29 "When Yahweh your God does cut off the nations—whither you are going in to possess them—from your presence, and you have possessed them, and have dwelt in their land —30 take heed to yourselves, lest you be snared after them, after their being destroyed out of your presence, and lest you inquire about their gods, saying, 'How do these nations serve their gods, that I may do so— even I?' 31 You do not do so to Yahweh your God; for every abomination to Yahweh which He hates they have done to their gods, for

even their sons and their daughters they burn with fire to their gods. ³² The whole thing which I am commanding you—it you observe to do; you do not add unto it, nor diminish from it."

(Deut. 12:28-32 NYLT)

Here we see Moses, in essence, saying that the holy books and oral traditions of other religions are incompatible with Holy Scripture and therefore are not to be assimilated with it. Similarly, Proverbs, chapter 30, beginning with verse 5 reads:

⁵ Every word of God is pure;
He is a shield to those who put their trust in Him.
⁶ Do not add to His words,
Lest He rebuke you, and you be found a liar.
(Prov. 30:5-6)

The Apostle Paul warns the Corinthian church in 1 Corinthians, "not to go beyond what is written" (4:6 ESV). Jude writes in the third verse of his epistle:

³ Beloved, while I was very diligent to write to you concerning our common salvation, I found it necessary to write to you exhorting you to contend earnestly for the faith which was once for all delivered to the saints.

(Jude 3)

Let me repeat that—"the faith which was once for all delivered to the saints." Not the faith that is still being divinely inspired or revealed to the saints. But the faith that has once for all time been delivered to the saints in the Holy Scriptures. We don't have to wait for new revelations. There are no new prophets. A modern Apostle does not exist. The canon of Scripture is once and for all closed, completed, and final. It consists of the 66 books of the Old and New Testaments and none other.

Finally, in Revelation, chapter 22, we read:

> 18 For I testify to everyone who hears the words of the prophecy of this book: If anyone adds to these things, God will add to him the plagues that are written in this book; 19 and if anyone takes away from the words of the book of this prophecy, God shall take away his part from the Book of Life, from the holy city, and from the things which are written in this book.
> (Rev. 22:18-19)

Concluding Implications:

There are other components or elements of *Sola Scriptura* that we could look at. We could look at its perspicuity—which means its ability to be read and understood by the common man. Jesus, for instance, repeatedly rebuked the religious hypocrites of His day, saying to them, "Have you not read in the book?" (Mk. 12:26; see also Matt. 12:3, 5, 19:4, 22:31; Mk. 12:10; Lk. 6:3) because it was so clearly understandable. As the great Reformation leader Martin Luther once said that, "A plowboy with a Bible knows more than the pope." We could also look at the power of God's Word—how it is living and powerful (Heb. 4:12; see also Jer. 23:29) and always accomplishes God's purposes (Is. 55:11). And there are others as well but, unfortunately, space will not permit us.

In conclusion, therefore, we have seen that this doctrine of *Sola Scriptura* is the first and most fundamental doctrine of our theology.   There are two massive implications that stem from this doctrine:

1. Supreme Authority.

First, that Holy Scriptures are the only supreme rule of faith and practice.   This means that all Church creeds, councils, and declarations have a lesser, subordinate authority than the authority of the Bible. Because Scripture alone is divinely inspired by God; because it alone is infallible or incapable of error; because it alone is inerrant or truthful, incapable of deceit; because it alone is immutable or unchangeable; because it alone is sufficient; because it alone is complete and final; it must alone be the supreme and final authority, judge, and arbitrator in matters of faith.

There is no other standard that even comes close. The decrees of the popes and councils of the Roman Catholic church are man-made and therefore certainly not divinely inspired or infallible.   Confessions of Faith, as beautiful and wonderful as they are in summarizing Biblical truth, are man-made and therefore is certainly not divinely inspired or infallible.   The statements of this religious leader or that religious conference are man-made and therefore certainly not divinely inspired or infallible.   And the words of preachers and pastors are man-made and therefore certainly not divinely inspired or infallible.

Rather, only the Bible satisfies the criteria of an objective, universal, and transcendent moral standard. Only the Bible, therefore, can bind the conscience.   Only the Bible can serve as the standard by which all creeds, councils, decrees, and opinions of men, no matter how wise and learned they may be, must be tried. The Bible alone is the essence of Truth and, therefore, it is the tribunal or judge of man-made claims to the truth.

Therefore, every opinion, feeling, thought, or attitude that I or anyone else has must be governed and subjected to the Word of God. I may think that my good works will save me, but because Scripture says that salvation is by grace alone through faith alone, it is my opinion, rather than the Bible, that must change. If I think that I become an angel when I die but Scripture says no such thing, then it is my opinion, rather than the Bible, that must change. If I call good what the Bible calls evil, and evil what the Bible calls good, it is my opinion, rather than the Bible, that must change. Because the Bible is the only God-breathed, infallible, inerrant divine authority in all matters upon which it touches: it is to be believed, as God's instruction, in all that it affirms; obeyed, as God's command, in all that it requires; and embraced, as God's pledge, in all that it promises.

Furthermore, when we are told that we must obey a papal decree, or a secular law, or Native religion that conflicts with the Bible, we are to, as the Apostles did long ago, reply that "We ought to obey God rather than men" (Acts 5:29). As Martin Luther proclaimed at the Diet of Worms when he was on trial for heresy before the Emperor of the Holy Roman Empire and faced execution by being burned at the stake:

> Unless you can convince me by Scripture...unless I am so convinced that I am wrong, I am bound to my beliefs by the text of the Bible. My conscience is captive to the word of God. To go against

conscience is neither right nor safe. Therefore I cannot and will not recant. Here I stand. I can do no other. God help me. Amen.

In conclusion, therefore, there is no other supreme authority for faith and conduct.

2. Exclusive Divine Revelation.

The second and related implication of *Sola Scriptura* is that the Bible is not only the supreme, but also the exclusive divine revelation of God's glory and man's salvation. Scripture alone is divinely inspired by God. Scripture alone is infallible or incapable of error. Scripture alone is inerrant or truthful, incapable of deceit. Scripture alone is immutable or unchangeable. Scripture alone is sufficient. Scripture alone is complete and final. And Scripture alone is the supreme and final authority, judge, and arbitrator in matters of faith. Therefore, only Scripture alone is God's inscripturated, special revelation; the exclusively sufficient, certain, complete, infallible, and necessary rule of all saving knowledge, faith, and obedience. It alone is the whole counsel of God concerning everything essential for His own glory and man's salvation, faith, and life.

For instance, the Apostle Paul proclaims in Romans 10:17 that, "faith [only] comes by the hearing, and hearing by the Word of God." In other words, mankind can only be saved through the exclusive message of the Bible and the Bible alone. This is because Jesus Himself declared in John 14:6 that, "I [alone] am the way, the truth, and the life, no man comes to the Father except through Me." Or as Peter put it in Acts, chapter 4:

> Nor is there salvation in any other, for there is no other name under heaven given among men by which we must be saved.
>
> (Acts 4:12)

The blood and righteousness of the God-man Jesus Christ is the exclusive means of salvation, and this message is contained exclusively in the Holy Scriptures. Therefore, Holy Scripture, and Holy Scripture alone, is the supreme, exclusive, and decisive Word of God concerning God's glory and man's salvation. There is no other sacred writing or oral tradition by which a man may be saved.

In Galatians, chapter 1, we find the Apostle Paul warning the churches among the Galatians:

> [6] I marvel that you are turning away so soon from Him who called you in the grace of Christ, to a different gospel, [7] which is not another; but there are some who trouble you and want to pervert the gospel of Christ. [8] But even if we, or an angel from heaven, preach any other gospel to you than what we have preached to you, let him be accursed. [9] As we have said before, so now I say again, if anyone preaches any other gospel to you than what you have received, let him be accursed.
>
> (Gal. 1:6-9)

What this means is that the only true, pure, and undefiled religion is found in the Bible. Any other religion, any other gospel, any other means of salvation, is a perverted falsehood.

What this means for our message as *martus* or witnesses for Christ is that we do not equivocate on the

20

supremacy and exclusivity of the Bible alone as the Word of God. All other so-called sacred writings, oral traditions, superstitions, and rituals and practices are false and lead to eternal death. When Christian missionaries came to my moon-worshipping ancestors in Europe centuries ago, they didn't say, "Oh, what a nice religion. Here's what we believe. Why don't we try to merge and assimilate the two?" No! They said, "Repent and believe the Bible (Mk. 1:15) or you are going to hell!"

Similarly, a missionary today to deepest darkest Africa, or the Native tribes in the jungles of South America, or the Tibetan highlands of China doesn't equivocate. He doesn't make nice. He does say, "You have your faith tradition and I have mine. That's cool, it's all relative." No! He says, "Repent and believe the Bible (Mk. 1:15) or you are going to hell!" He warns the Muslim that there is no such thing as a paradise full of 70 virgins for blowing yourself up as an Islamic terrorist. He tells the Hindu that there is no such thing as being reincarnation into a better you. He tells the Buddhist that there is no such thing as achieving nirvana. And he tells the Native American that there is no such thing as happy hunting grounds.

And his authority for doing so is not his own but rather it is derived from the Word of God. Therefore, he proclaims to them there is only one God, the God of Scripture alone. That there is only one heaven, the heaven of Scripture alone. That there is only one hell, the hell of Scripture alone. That there is only one moral code by which we are to live, and that is the moral code of Scripture alone. And that there is only one Savior and Redeemer—the Lord Jesus Christ of Scripture and Scripture alone. And that there is only one way of salvation, and that is in Scripture and Scripture alone.

This is our emphatic and unequivocal message—that all kingdoms and nations, cultures and traditions, rituals and practices, must and will bow the knee to God and His Word in the Bible. Holy Scripture is irreconcilable with any other religion. Holy Scripture is incompatible with any other religion. Holy Scripture is intolerant of any other religion.

But the religion of the Bible is also the most loving religion in the world, for it alone will hazard everything to tell a people group—at risk of life, limb, and reputation— that they are wrong and going to hell but that the Bible offers them the only means of eternal life. The adherents of no other religion would endure, joyfully and gladly, martyrdom for such a witness, but we would.

The authenticity of *Sola Scriptura*—that Scripture alone is divinely inspired; infallible or incapable of error; inerrant or truthful, incapable of deceit; immutable or unchangeable; sufficient; complete and final; and supreme and exclusive—is attested to by the blood of countless thousands of martyrs over the past 2,000 years. That is our heritage. That is our witness.

2 SOLA GRATIA

*I*n this chapter we will turn our attention to the second Reformation *Sola—Sola Gratia*—the doctrine that salvation is by grace alone. There are many, many verses in the Bible that speak to the fact that salvation is by God's grace and God's grace alone. Romans 3:24, for instance, proclaims that we are, "justified freely by [God's] grace through the redemption that is in Christ Jesus." Or Acts 15:11 reads, "But we believe that through the grace of the Lord Jesus Christ we shall be saved..." Ephesians 1:7 declares that, "in Him [Jesus Christ] we have redemption through His blood, the forgiveness of sins, according to the riches of His grace." And, finally, perhaps the most famous verse on grace of all, Ephesians 2:8 proclaims, "For by grace you have been saved through faith, and that not of yourselves, it is the gift of God" (see also 2:5).

But what is grace? We often hear the phrase, "Mercy is *not* getting what we do deserve, while grace *is* getting what we do not deserve." Or another term for grace is unearned or unmerited favor. The Greek word translated *grace* in the New Testament is *charis*, which means kindness or favor. What we mean, therefore, when we say that salvation is by God's grace alone is that it is an unmerited gift of God by which He not only pardons us and reconciles us to Him, but by which we enter into life and fellowship with God, both in this life and in the one to come.

Another way of putting it is that grace alone means that salvation is monergistic—that God alone is the only effectual actor in our salvation. God's grace is not synergistic—it does not depend on our will, merit, or actions for its success. Rather, God alone acts in our redemption, and He does so effectively and decisively without any contributing effort on our part. For we not only do not deserve God's grace but, left to our own desires and devices, we are incapable of cooperating with it whatsoever.

Today, therefore, we are first going to magnify God's grace by seeing just how unmerited it is, then we are going to break down our salvation from start to finish to see how, from Scripture, it is entirely God-sided.

1. Unmerited Favor.

The first essential component of grace alone is that it is entirely and completely an act of unmerited favor. We will never understand God, ourselves, or our salvation until we understand the holiness of God. In the beginning, before anything else—whether time, dimension, or molecules—God alone was. God alone existed. God alone had life. God alone thought, and loved, and acted. In the most important passage on God's holiness in the entire Bible, we read:

> [13] And Moses said unto God, "Behold!—I am coming unto the sons of Israel, and have said to them, 'The God of your fathers has sent me unto you,' and they have said to me, 'What is His name?' what do I say unto them?"
> [14] And God said unto Moses, "I AM WHO I AM." He said also, "You shall say to the sons of Israel, 'I AM has sent me unto you.'"
> [15] And God said again unto Moses, "Thus you shall say unto the sons of Israel: 'Yahweh God of your fathers—God of Abraham, God of Isaac, and God of Jacob—has sent me unto

you. This is My name—to the age; and this My memorial—from generation to generation.'"

(Ex. 3:13-15 NYLT)

Notice the three names God uses in these verses:
- **Verse 14:** I AM WHO I AM
- **Verse 14:** I AM
- **Verse 15:** Yahweh

All three are used interchangeably as the name of the God who is sending Moses to Pharaoh (vs. 14-15), and all three share the same Hebrew root *hayah*, which simply means *to be*. There is no more profound declaration than that—"I AM WHO I AM" (Ex. 3:14-15). The God of the Bible, therefore, is the Great I AM—the uncreated, self-sufficient, self-existent, unchangeable, limitless One who has no beginning, no end, no need, and no weakness (Ex. 3:14-15; Numb. 23:19; Ps. 33:11, 102:27; Mal. 3:6; Jn. 5:26; Heb. 13:8; Jac. 1:17; Rev.1:8, 22:13). No one made God. He is life in Himself. He is not dependent on anyone or anything else. He has no limit. He exists outside of time. And He cannot be improved upon because He has always been infinitely perfect. Neither Allah, nor or the gods of Hindu, nor Wakanda, nor Zeus, nor Jupiter, nor any other so-called god can make such a claim, but only the Great I AM Yahweh. God must, by very definition, be holy.

In Isaiah, chapter 6, we read:

> 1 In the year of the death of King Uzziah, I see Adonai sitting on a throne, high and lifted up, and His train is filling the temple.
> 2 Seraphs are standing above it: six wings has each one; with two each covers its

face, and with two each covers its feet,
and with two each flies. ³ And this one
has called unto that *one* and has said:
"Holy, Holy, Holy, is Yahweh Sabaoth!
The fulness of all the earth is His glory!"

(Is. 6:1-3 NYLT)

In this passage the word *holy* is used three times,
which is a Hebrew literary device to emphasis the
weightiness and magnitude of the word.   Here the
seraphim thrice cried out, "Holy, holy, holy" (Is. 6:3) to
stress the infinite and unsurpassed holiness of Yahweh
Sabaoth. God's holiness is to the superlative degree—His
holiness is perfect, unable to be improved upon, and
shared by no rival.

Again, in Revelation, chapter 4, we find the Apostle
John describing a vision of Yahweh:

¹ After these things I saw and behold!—a door
opened in the heaven, and the first voice that I
heard is as of a trumpet speaking with me,
saying, "Come up here, and I will show you
what of necessity must come to pass after
these things." ² And immediately I was in the
Spirit, and behold!—a throne was set in the
heaven, and upon the throne is One sitting.
³ And He who is sitting was in appearance like
a stone—jasper and sardius—and a rainbow
was round the throne in appearance like an
emerald.

⁴ And around the throne are twenty-four
thrones, and upon the thrones I saw the
twenty-four elders sitting, clothed in white
garments, and they had upon their heads

crowns of gold.   5 And out of the throne proceed lightnings, and thunderings, and voices; and seven lamps of fire are burning before the throne, which are the Seven Spirits of God.

6 And before the throne is a sea of glass like unto crystal, and in the midst of the throne, and round the throne, are four living creatures, full of eyes before and behind.   7 And the first living creature is like a lion, and the second living creature is like a calf, and the third living creature hath the face as a man, and the fourth living creature is like an eagle flying.   8 And the four living creatures, one for one of them had, respectively, had six wings, around and within are full of eyes, and rest they have not day and night, saying:

"Holy, holy, holy,
Lord God Almighty,
who was, and who is, and who is coming!"

9 And when the living creatures do give glory, and honor, and thanks, to Him who is sitting upon the throne, who is living to the ages of the ages, 10 the twenty-four elders do fall down before Him who is sitting upon the throne, and bow before Him who is living to the ages of the ages, and they cast their crowns before the throne, saying,

11 "Worthy are You, O Lord,
to receive the glory, and the honor, and the power,
because You did create the all things,
And because of Your will they are, and they were created."

27

(Rev. 4:1-11 NYLT)

Holiness refers to Yahweh's uniqueness, His utter set-apartness from anything or anyone else. It is the magisterial perfection of all His attributes—His love, mercy, grace, anger, wrath, justice, faithfulness, righteousness, goodness, sovereignty, all-powerfulness, omnipresence, all-knowing, and wisdom, to name but a few.

The term *holiness* refers to Yahweh's intrinsic value and worth; the essential or innate splendor and beauty of being God. Necessary to His essence, therefore, is that Yahweh is the most supremely valuable Being imaginable in the magisterial perfection of all His attributes which He exercises in perfect harmony one with the other. Yahweh is all His attributes all the time in all that He does for all eternity. Therefore, He alone is the source of infinite joy and delight for mankind.

And this God who dwells in unapproachable light (1 Tim. 6:16), is the creator and sustainer of everything that is, and was, and is to come, both visible and invisible (Gen. 1; John 1:1-3; Heb. 11:1). He created the universe out of nothing (Heb. 11:1) and upholds every second of its existence by His word (Neh. 9:6; Col. 1:15-17). He has set the sun, moon, and stars in their orbits, and they obeyed Him. He has set planets, and black holes, and galaxies in their place, and they obeyed Him (Job 38-41; Ps. 104). He told the mountains to rise up, and they obeyed Him (Ibid.). He told the valleys to form, and they obeyed Him (Ibid.). He told the oceans to come this far and no further, and they obeyed Him (Ibid.).

Every single day, He designs the sunrise and sunset for our enjoyment (Job 38-41; Ps. 104). Every single night, He paints the tapestry of the stars for us to gaze at in amazement (Ibid.). Every single day He feeds the animals

(Job 38:39-41; Ps. 104:13, 21, 27-30) and determines when they take their last breath (Ps. 104:29-30; Matt. 10:29; Lk. 12:6). Every single day He takes up His pen to write a new act for creation to follow (Job 38-41; Ps. 104).

As Moses sang in Exodus 15 after Yahweh brought His people Israel out of captivity in Egypt:

> Who is like You among the gods, O Yahweh?
> Who is like You, glorious in holiness,
> Fearful in praises, doing wonders?
> (Ex. 15:11 NYLT)

Hannah declared in 1 Samuel 2:2 that, "There is none holy like Yahweh! For there is none save You, and there is no rock like our God!" (NYLT). God Himself declares, "'To whom then will you liken Me. Or to whom shall I be equal?" says the Holy One' (Is. 40:25). Or as He says elsewhere, "'I am God, and not man. The Holy One in your midst'" (Hos. 11:9). God is incomprehensible in His terrible, unique beauty. As the psalmist declares:

> 4 High above all nations is Yahweh! Above the heavens is His glory! 5 Who is as Yahweh our God—He is exalting Himself to sit *enthroned on high*, 6 *yet* He is humbling Himself to look on the heavens and on the earth?
> (Psalm 113:4-6 NYLT)

This God is deserving of all of our praise, all our worship, all our adoration, all our love, and all our mind. But, beginning with the first man Adam and his wife Eve, mankind's problem is that we want to be gods rather than submit to God. We find in Genesis, chapter 2, that God gave our first man Adam a covenant of works that consisted of but a single commandment:

> 16 And Yahweh God lays a charge on the man, saying, "Of every tree of the garden eating you eat, 17 but of the tree of knowledge of good and evil, you do not eat of it, for in the day of your eating of it—dying you do die."
>
> (Gen. 2:16-17 NYLT)

But we read in Genesis 3 that: "4 Then the serpent said to the woman, 'You will not surely die. 5 For God knows that in the day you eat of it your eyes will be opened, and you will be like God, knowing good and evil'" (Gen. 3:4-5). And the very next verse tells us that the first man Adam and his wife Eve believed the devil's lie and ate the forbidden fruit because they desired to be like God in His wisdom—judging for themselves what is good and evil. And when they did so, the Bible tells us that they inherited eternal death (Rom. 6:23) though they continued, for a time, to physically live (1 Tim. 5:6).

Mankind's problem, therefore, is that in the *very same sin* that Adam sinned, all mankind sinned as well. Romans, chapter 5, makes this explicitly clear:

> Therefore, just as sin entered the world through one man, and death through sin, and in this way death came to all men, because *all sinned*.
>
> (Rom. 5:12 NIV84; emphasis added)

We see this confirmed five other places throughout the fifth chapter of Romans:

30

- **Verse 15:** By "the one man [Adam's] offense many died."
- **Verse 16:** "[T]he judgment which came from one offense resulted in condemnation."
- **Verse 17:** "[B]y the one man [Adam's] offense death reigned through the one."
- **Verse 18:** "[T]hrough one man [Adam's] offense judgment came to all men, resulting in condemnation."
- **Verse 19:** "[B]y one man [Adam's] disobedience many were made sinners."

Let me restate these five verses in reverse order to help make it clearer: (1) by the *very same* sin of our first parent Adam, all humanity was made—or imputed—to have committed the same sin as well (vs. 19); and therefore (2) all men are imputed from the moment of conception to be as guilty and unrighteous as Adam and consequently under God's rightful judgment (vs. 18) and condemnation (vs. 16, 18); which (3) resulted in both physical and spiritual death for all men (vs. 15, 17; see also 1 Cor. 15:45-49).

Our first man Adam was our federal head. Much like an agent binds the principal, or a politician the constituents he represents, so Adam's actions were legally binding on his progeny. In the case of the covenant of works which God imposed on Adam, God viewed humanity as a corporate entity represented by its first parent. As a result, mankind inherited not only the sin of the first man Adam, but also his eternal punishment and corrupted sin nature.

For the Bible tells us that we are not born as an innocent blank slate free to choose whether to be either good or bad. Rather, as a descendent of the first man Adam, we have had our sin nature from the moment of our conception.   In Psalm 51:5, for instance, the psalmist declares, "Surely I was sinful at birth, sinful from the time my mother conceived me." In Psalm 58:3 we read, "Even from birth the wicked go astray; from the womb they are wayward and speak lies." Therefore, the problem we have is not that we commit sins, but that we are sinful. We are not a sinner because we commit sins, we commit sins because we are a sinner.

Therefore, by this inherited corruption we have received from Adam, our very nature is sin. Not merely our actions, thoughts, or behaviors, but we ourselves are sin. Our soul is black as night and uglier than hell. We have been as grotesque in our evil as any demon of hell from the moment we were conceived and therefore have always been under the rightful sentence of eternal damnation. This is why we sin—because we were a sinner from conception. This is why we cannot stop sinning—because we were a sinner from conception. This is why we will die a physical death—because we were a sinner from conception. This is why, apart from a Savior, we will roast for all eternity in hell—because we were a sinner from conception.

Furthermore, we not only sinned in the first man Adam's sin, but we also commit our own sins every single second of every single day of our entire lives.   For Romans, chapter 3, declares that:

> 9 What, then? Are we better? Not at all! For we did previously charge both Jews and Greeks with being all under sin.
> 10 According as it has been written:
> "There is none righteous, not even one;
> 11 There is none who is understanding,
> There is none who is seeking after God.

12 All did go out of the way,
Together they became unprofitable;
There is none doing good, there is not even one."...
18 "There is no fear of God before their eyes."...
23 for all did sin, and are come short of the glory of God...

(Rom. 3:9-12, 18, 23 NYLT)

In Mark 10:18, Jesus told the right young ruler that "no one is good but One, that is, God." The Apostle John writes, "Whoever commits sin also commits lawlessness, and sin is lawlessness" (1 Jn. 3:4). From birth we have rejected and ridiculed God's right to govern our lives as we blasphemously declare to Him, "Not Your will be my will be done!" We are in a state of insurrection, of rebellion, in which the Bible tells us that everyone does what is right in his own eyes (Num. 15:39; Deut. 12:8; Judges 17:6, 21:25).

All of us sin. All the time. Without stop. And we are incapable of doing anything other than sin. We are hardwired to sin and cannot stop doing it. We have become it's slave for, as Jesus said in John 8:34, "'Most assuredly I say to you, whoever commits sin is a slave of sin.'" Or as the Apostle John tells us in his first epistle, "He who sins is of the devil, for the devil has sinned from the beginning...Whoever sins has neither seen God nor known Him" (1 John 3:8, 6). Genesis 6:5 declares that, "...the wickedness of man [i]s great in the earth, and that every intent of the thoughts of his heart [i]s only evil continually."

And because of this inherited guilt and corruption we received from Adam, the Bible declares us to be spiritually dead. The Apostle Paul, for instance, tells us in Romans

8:6 that, "The mind of the sinful man is *death*" (Rom. 8:6). In Ephesians 2, in both verses 1 and 5 Paul declares that, "you were *dead* in your transgressions and sins" (emphasis added). IThe Scripture tells us that, "you were *dead* in your sins and in the uncircumcision of your sinful nature" (Col. 2:13; emphasis added). In His parable of the Prodigal Son, Jesus describes the returning prodigal as one who "was *dead* but is alive again" (Lk. 15:24, 32; emphasis added (see also 1 Jn. 3:14)).

Our souls are spiritual corpses. Our hearts are dead to the light and beauty of God. We have no capacity to love, treasure, or worship God. We are nothing more than stiffs at the morgue. We can no more respond to God than a dead man talk or see. From the moment of conception we have been dead spiritually though we live physically (1 Tim. 5:6). We, very much, are the walking dead. And we are spiritually dead and are completely powerless to make ourselves anything but spiritually dead. We are dead. We like our deadness. And we hate life. And, left to our own desires and devices, we are completely incapable of either wanting to or of in fact raising ourselves from the dead.

2. God Alone—Monergism.

Fallen mankind is part of a bad tree in which we have inherited the guilt, death, and sin nature of our first man Adam. By this inherited corruption we have received from Adam, we are utterly biased against, and disabled and antagonistic toward, God. We have, since birth, been children of lawlessness who can no more do good than an apple tree produce oranges or a dalmatian change its spots.

Consequently, it is impossible for us to make ourselves good enough to receive salvation. It is impossible for us to make ourselves good enough to keep salvation. It is impossible for us to have any self-righteousness before salvation. And it is impossible for us to have any self-righteousness after salvation. We cannot—in whole or in part—save ourselves. God owes us nothing for any past "good works" we may have done. Rather, we are pure evil and wickedly corrupt and can have no hope of ever earning God's favor. Our very nature is one of sinful blasphemy against a holy and righteous God, and it cannot be atoned for by tears, resolutions, good works, legalism, or any other effort on our part. God owes us nothing but eternal damnation from the moment we were conceived, and it is the height of pompous arrogance for sinful mankind to presume that a just and pure God owes them anything.

This is what is meant, therefore by *Sola Gratia*—that if we are to be saved from our spiritual deadness and eternal damnation, it must be by God's grace and God's grace alone. For if God will not redeem us, there is no other conceivable Savior to rescue us. Not us. Not our parents or spouse. Not even the archangels of heaven are able to impart spiritual life. Only God, in showing us unearned and unmerited favor, is able to save us and sanctify us. And He does so as the only effectual and decisive actor in our salvation with no contribution on our part.

In Romans, chapter 8, we read:

> [29] For whom He foreknew, He also predestined to be conformed to the image of His Son, that He might be the firstborn among many brethren. [30] Moreover whom He predestined, these He also called; whom He called, these He also justified; and whom He justified, these He also glorified.

(Rom. 8:29-30)

Notice all the "He's" used in these two verses. "He foreknew." "He predestined." "He called." "He justified." "He...glorified." This is why the Bible calls salvation an act of God's grace from start to finish. Let's examine these five stages one at a time.

Foreknew. First, "He foreknew." "Foreknew" here is another term for *choosen* or *elected*. If anyone is to be saved, it must be by God's choice and God's choice alone. God has chosen a people for Himself from out of fallen humanity before the creation of the world, and such election was completely and entirely sovereign, free, and unconditional. By *unconditional*, we mean that the basis or reasons for God's election are owing to nothing in an individual whatsoever. By God's sovereign and independent choice, He could have saved Hitler and damned Mother Theresa. By their works, no one has a claim on HIs grace, and no one is beyond His grace.

The Apostle Paul ells us that God "choose"—or foreknew, foreloved, or elected—the regenerate "in Him [Christ Jesus] before the foundation of the world" (Eph. 1:4). In Jesus said that, "'All that the Father gives Me will come to Me, and the one who comes to Me I will by know means cast out'" (Jn. 6:37) and, again, that, "'Therefore I have said to you that no one can come to Me unless it has been given to him by My father'" (vs. 65). A few chapters later Jesus said that, "'I know whom I have chosen'" (Jn. 13:18), and Paul tells us in 2 Timothy that, "the solid foundation of God stands, having this seal: 'The Lord knows those who are His'" (2 Tlm. 2:19).

Turn with me to Romans, chapter 9, where we find God's foreknowing—or choosing, or election, or foreloving—clearing established by the Apostle Paul:

- **Verse 11:** "[F]or the children not yet being born, nor having done any good or evil, that the purpose of God according to election might stand." In other words, God's electing purpose—established before we are born and have done any good or evil—will not and cannot be thwarted or added by our behavior or actions.
- **Verse 11:** Foreknowing—or foreloving, election, or choose—is "not of works but of Him who calls."
- **Verse 16:** "So then it is not of him who wills, nor of him who runs, but of God who shows mercy."
- **Verse 18:** "Therefore He has mercy on whom He wills, and whom He wills He hardens."

As God told Moses in Exodus 33: "'I cause all My goodness to pass before your face, and have called concerning the Name of Yahweh before you, and favored him whom I favor, and loved him whom I love'" (Ex. 33:19 NYLT). The Apostle Paul tells us in Ephesians 5 that God has a Bride—the church—whom He "gave Himself for [] that He might sanctify and cleanse her with the washing of water and the word" (Eph. 5:25-26). And God foreknew—or foreloved, chose, or elected—this Bride owing to nothing in her. It would be like an unmarried President of the United States or billionaire walking blindfolded into the mall and suddenly picking a woman at random to marry. He isn't doing so because of any worth on her part. He doesn't know anything about her, even what she looks like. He just arbitrarily picked her for reasons known only to him and not for any merit she might have.

Similarly, God so foreknew—or foreloved, choose, elected—His Bride. Foreknowing, therefore, is the free act of the sovereign God in which from eternity past (Eph. 1:4, 11), for reasons known only to Himself (Matt. 11:27), and apart from any foreseen faith and/or goodness found in her (Rom. 8:29-30, 9:11; 2 Tim. 1:9), He graciously chose from among the fallen mankind a people unto salvation that they might be conformed to the image of Christ (Eph. 4:13). In ages past, before the creation of the world and anyone was born or had done a single deed, whether good or bad, God sovereignly, freely, and unconditionally chose from among a humanity—blind, hardened, and dead in their sinful nature—those who would receive the Gospel and thereby be undeservedly saved for all eternity and who would remain a rebel against God and thereby be deservedly damned for all eternity. You do not make yourself a Christian, but rather God makes you a Christian because He choose to do so before time even began. You are not elect by God because He foresaw that you would believe; rather, you believe because you are the elect of God.

Predestined. Secondly, God predestined. God's foreknowing—or foreloving, choosing, or election—is often used interchangeably with the term predestination. However, here in Romans 8:29-30, Paul is using the term predestination to refer specifically to the goal or end of God's foreknowing—namely, that we are to be conformed to the image of His Son. In Ephesians 1, we are told that God "predestined us to adoption as sons by Jesus Christ to Himself" (Eph. 1:5). And in verse 11 tells us that believers are predestined to obtain an inheritance "according to the purpose of Him who works all things according to the counsel of His will" (vs. 11). And all this, we are told, with the ultimate goal of being "to the praise of the glory of His grace" (vs. 6 (see also vs. 7, 12).

Consequently, God irrevocably foreknows—or foreloves, chooses, or elects—the elect to *the predestined end that* we should be His Bride, His children, His inheritance "to the praise of his glory" (vs. 12). Going back to the analogy of the unmarried man in the mall randomly picking a woman to marry. Foreknowing—or foreloving, choosing, or electing—refers to his decision to marry her, while predestination refers to ends for which he did so—to make her his one and only bride to love and to cherish and to raise a family.

Called. Third, God calls. Jesus tells us that, "'He who is of God hears God's words; therefore you do not hear because you are not of God'" (Jn. 8:46-47). If a person is foreknown and predestined by God, they will hear God's regenerating call upon their hearts. Again, a few chapters later in John Jesus tells us that, "'My sheep hear my voice, and I know them, and they follow me'" (Jn. 10:27). We see the same thing over and over again in just the Gospel of John alone:

- **John 6:37:** "All that the Father does give Me will come to Me, and him who is coming unto Me I will by no means cast without" (NYLT).
- **John 6:44:** "No one is able to come unto Me if the Father who sent Me does not irresistibly drags him; and I will raise him up in the last day" (NYLT).
- **John 6:45:** "...'Everyone therefore who heard from the Father, and learned, comes to Me'" (NYLT).
- **John 6:65:** "...'Because of this I have said to you— no one is able to come unto Me if it may not have been granted him from My Father'" (NYLT).

• **John 8:42:** "...'If God were your father, you were loving Me, for I came forth from God, and am come, for neither have I come of Myself but He sent Me'" (NYLT).

In other words, only those who have been born again can love Christ; those still dead in their trespasses and sins (Eph. 2:1) cannot love Christ to accept Him, receive Him, or treasure Him.

The Father gives (Jn. 6:37, 65). The Father irresistibly drags (6:44). The Father calls and teaches (6:45). You are not the effectual and decisive agent in your salvation; God is. You did not become a Christian because you were smart enough to figure it out. You did not become a Christian because you mustered up enough faith. You did not become a Christian because you willed it and made a decision. Remember that we are spiritually dead—blind and hardened in our deadness—who are rebels against God. We have been conceived with a sin nature of inborn, spiteful rebellion against God in which we hate Him, loath Him, flee from Him, deny Him, and want nothing to do with Him. He has no beauty to us but only serves to show us how filthy we really are (Jn. 3:19-20). As a result, the Good News of Calvary is laughable to us in our fallen state (1 Cor. 1:18-31, 2:14).

Therefore, the only reason you became a Christian is because God foreknew you, predestined you, and then called you. As the Apostle Paul tells us: "For it is the God who commanded light to shine out of darkness [at the moment of creation], who has shone in our hearts to give the light of the glory of God in the face of Jesus Christ" (2 Cor. 4:6). In other words, just as God created the universe out of nothing, so at the moment of His calling He creates a living, fleshly, seeing heart out of a blind, hardened, dead spiritual corpse. We see this, for instance, in the

40

description of Lydia's conversion at Philippi, where we are told that, "The Lord opened her heart to heed the things spoken by Paul" (Acts 16:14). Notice that Lydia didn't open her own heart, but that the Lord opened her heart for her (see also Matt. 16:13-17).

Like Jesus crying out, "Come forth!" in front of Lazarus' tomb and the dead man suddenly walked out (Jn. 11:43), God's effectual and decisive call regenerates or rebirths (Jn. 3:3) a spiritually dead rebel—blind and hardened in their deadness—into a new creation (2 Cor. 5:17) in which they now love the God they once hated and hate the sin they once loved. By this saving, regenerating call of God, the dead now live, the blind now see, the deaf now hear, and the unbelieving now believe.

Returning once again to the analogy, the woman at the mall initially didn't find the man attractive at all. She thought he was ugly, boring, and repugnant. She thought that he was a goody-too-shoes who would cramp her style. But when he proposed and she heard his voice, her heart was instantaneously changed anew and she suddenly found him irresistibly beautiful. His love for her flooded her heart and she couldn't help but say "yes" as she eagerly grasped at the ring he offered her. Her will became captive to his love as she found herself delighting in loving, honoring, and cherishing him until death do them part.

Justified. Fourth, God alone justifies. Romans 3:24 declares that we are, "justified freely by His grace through the redemption that is in Christ Jesus." Our justification is past-tense. It is a completed legal verdict that took place outside of ourselves on a hill called Calvary when Christ, who knew no sin, was made a sin offering for us so that we, who had no righteousness, might live in His righteousness (2 Cor. 5:12). And this forensic justification, this verdict of righteousness, wrought by Christ's substitutionary atonement upon the cross, is imputed to us by the agency of faith at the moment of our salvation.

As Ezekiel the prophet tells us, God has "cleanse[d] you from all your impurities and from all your idols...save[d] you from all your uncleanness" (Ezek. 36:25, 29a). Or as Psalm 103:12 declares, "[A]s far as the east is from the west, so far has He removed our transgressions from us!" The famous hymn *It Is Well With My Soul* describes it this transaction so well:

> That Christ has regarded my helpless
> estate
> And has shed His own blood for my
> soul...
> My sin, oh the bliss of this glorious
> thought
> My sin, not in part, but the whole
> Is nailed to the cross, and I bear it no
> more
> Praise the Lord, praise the Lord, O my
> soul

By faith in Christ, all of our sin—past, present, and future—is nailed to the cross and we bear it no more! What a freeing, liberating, glorious thought indeed! Therefore—justified by Christ's blood, clothed with His righteousness—your past failures do not define you. Your current temptations do not define you. Your present circumstances do not define you. Rather, in coming to God in penitent faith, only Christ and His redeeming and purifying love now defines you! His banner over you is now love (Song of Solomon 2:4)! He now surrounds you with songs of deliverance (Ps. 32:7)! He now rejoices over you with gladness (Is. 62:4-5; Zeph. 3:17)! He now quiets you with His love (Zeph. 3:17)! He now rejoices over you with singing (Zeph. 3:17)!

And this can only be the result of free, unmerited, unearnable, unfathomable grace. For in Ezekiel 36:32, God tells us that He does this, "'Not for your sake,' an affirmation of Adonai Yahweh. 'Rather, be it known to you, be ashamed and confounded because of your ways...'" (NYLT). Ephesians declares that, "He predestined us for adoption as sons through Jesus Christ, according to the purpose of His will, *for the praise of the glory of His grace*" (Eph. 1:5-6; emphasis added). Again, in Ezekiel God declares:

> "22 Therefore, say to the house of Israel, 'Thus said Adonai Yahweh: "Not for your sake am I working, O house of Israel, but for My holy name that you have polluted among nations whither you have gone in.   23 And I have sanctified My great name that is profaned among nations, that you have polluted in your midst, and the nations have that I am Yahweh...""
>
> (Ezek. 36:22-23 NYLT)

And yet in another place He tells us that, "I am He who blots out your transgressions for My own sake, and I will not remember your sins" (Is. 43:25).

Returning to our analogy of the man in the mall—the woman he proposed to was a murderer. And not just any murderer, but the murderer of his first wife. She was moments away from being arrested, tried, convicted, and summarily executed. But the man and his one and only son willingly, freely, and unconditionally agreed that the son would be executed in her place. The son did so, the woman was declared forensically innocent, and there now remained no barrier between marriage for this man and his most unworthy, unlovable bride.

Glorified. Fifth and finally, God alone glorifies His elect Bride. Or, to put it another way, God will preserve His elect children until their final breath when they will join Him in His glory. In Romans, chapter 8, we find the Apostle Paul exclaiming:

> 31 What, then, shall we say unto these things? If God is for us, who is against us? 32 He who indeed His own Son did not spare, but for us all did deliver Him up, how shall He not also with Him grant all things to us? 33 Who shall lay a charge against the elect of God? God is He that is declaring righteous. 34 Who is he that is condemning? Christ is He that died, yes, rather also, was raised up; who is also on the right hand of God, who also does intercede for us. 35 Who shall separate us from the love of the Messiah—tribulation, or distress, or persecution, or famine, or nakedness, or peril, or sword 36 (according as it has been written , "For You sake we are put to death all the day long, we were reckoned as sheep of slaughter")? 37 But in all these we more than conquer through Him who loved us. 38 For I am persuaded that neither death, nor life, nor *angelic* messengers, nor principalities, nor powers, nor things present, 39 nor things about to be, nor

height, nor depth, nor any other created thing, shall be able to separate us from the love of God, that is in Messiah Jesus our Lord.

(Rom. 8:31-39 NYLT)

As Jesus declared in the Gospel of John: "[25]...I am the resurrection and the life. He who believes in Me, though he may die, he shall live. [26] And whoever lives and believes in Me shall never die..." (Jn. 11:25-26). Or as Jesus told Nicodemus in the most famous verse of the Bible: "'For God so loved the world that He gave His only begotten Son, that whoever believes in Him should not perish but have everlasting life.'" (Jn. 3:16).

John the Witness declares that, "He who believes in the Son has everlasting life" (Jn. 3:36). The Apostle Paul tells us that, "if we died with Christ, we believe that we will also live with Him" (Rom. 6:8 (see also 2 Tim. 2:11)). Or as he put it elsewhere, Christ "died for us, that whether we wake or sleep [i.e., die], we should live together with Him" (1 Thess. 5:10). "And so we will always be with the Lord" (1 Thess. 4:17).

In Christ by faith, you are clothed with His righteousness, engulfed by God's love, and that can never be shaken, altered, or destroyed in any way! You are His Bride, now and forever. You live in Christ, you will die in Christ, and you will spend an eternity of eternities with Christ! There are no dropouts in this unbreakable chain of God's electing and persevering love described for us here in Romans 8:29-30!

Returning to the man in the mall analogy, divorce between the couple is not an option. A worldwide law was passed declaring that this man and his bride were irrevocably joined until death do them part, that any divorce

45

decree would be legally null and void, and that any judge issuing such a decree would be tortured to death. Their marriage vows were, literally, unbreakable and unalterable. They were partners for life—for better or for worse, for richer or for poorer. Till death do them part.

Concluding Implications:

In conclusion, therefore, we have seen that salvation is, from start to finish, an act of God's unearned, unmerited favor. He initiated it. He implemented it. He obtained it. He applies it. He guarantees it. And He will complete it until the very end. As Jacob tells us, "Of His own will He brought us forth by the word of truth..." (Jac. 1:18). The only thing we contribute to our salvation is our sin. That's it. That is what is meant when we say that salvation is by God's grace and God's grace alone.

To say otherwise would be blasphemy. It would make God less holy than He is, it would make our sin and depravity less serious than they are, and it would make the sacrifice of God's one and only Son upon the cross a cheap trinket rather than the priceless treasure it truly is. Grace alone, therefore, is at the very heart of the Gospel message. Any other message puts man in the driver's seat of his own salvation. It makes God serve man rather than man serve God. It makes man his savior rather than God. Only the message of grace alone shatters man's pride and magnifies God's glory. Only it puts us in our rightful lowly and humble station and exalts God to His rightful position as our Lord who indeed is mighty to save. To God alone be all the glory, great things He alone has done!

3 SOLA FIDE (PART ONE)

*I*n this chapter we are going to examine the doctrine of *Sola Fide*—that justification is by faith alone. There are four questions that we must address. First, what is justification? Secondly, how do we make this justification ours? Third, does faith excludes works? Fourth and finally, is this faith by which alone we are justified in fact a work or a gift?

I. **Justification = to be Declared Righteous.**

The first question, therefore, is what does it mean to be justified? Or, to put it another way, how can a sinful, vile, impure man become right with a holy and righteous God? As Job desperately asks, "how can a man be righteous before God?" (Job 9:2). This is the central question nearly all religions of the world seek to answer. This is the essential question that all human beings should be haunted with until they have, in the light of Scripture, satisfactorily answered it. For because there is a holy and pure God before whom we must one day give an account, we should dread the coming of that Day of Judgment with much fear and trembling. As the Bible declares in Romans, even our consciences bear witness against us and condemn us before God's perfect law (Rom. 2:15).

Romans, chapters 1 and 2, spell out God's indictment against all humanity. Romans 2:1 warns us that, "[Y]ou are inexcusable, O man" for the sin which you willfully embrace because you know God's character and His moral law. All men are without excuse, for in giving us both the intellectual design of nature (Rom. 1:19-20) and a moral conscience (Rom. 2:15), these passages declare that God has revealed:

1. the knowledge of Himself (Rom. 1:21, 28),
2. "the glory of the Incorruptible God" (vs. 23),
3. the "truth of God" (vs. 25), and
4. the "righteous judgments of God" (vs. 32).

Therefore, God declares that all men everywhere "are without excuse" (Rom. 1:20) because even though they knew God's revelation of Himself in nature and on their consciences, they:

1. "Suppressed the truth in unrighteousness" (Rom. 1:18).
2. "They did not glorify Him as God, nor were thankful, but they become futile in their thoughts and their foolish hearts were darkened" (vs. 21).
3. "22 Professing to be wise, [they] became fools 23 by changing the glory of the incorruptible God into an image made like corruptible man—and birds and four-footed animals and creeping things" (vs. 22-23).
4. "They exchanged the truth of God for the lie, and worshiped and served the creature rather than the Creator, who is blessed forever" (vs. 25).
5. "They did not like to retain God in their knowledge" (vs. 28).

In Romans, chapter 3, we find God's verdict on fallen humanity:

9 What, then? Are we better? Not at all! For we did previously charge both Jews and Greeks with being all under sin.
10 According as it has been written:
"There is none righteous, not even one;

> [11] There is none who is understanding,
> There is none who is seeking after God.
> [12] All did go out of the way,
> Together they became unprofitable;
> There is none doing good, there is not even one."...
> [18] "There is no fear of God before their eyes."...
> [23] for all did sin, and are come short of the glory of God...
>
> (Rom. 3:9-12, 18, 23 NYLT)

All men everywhere have no choice but to echo Ezra in declaring, "Here we are before You in our guilt, though because of it no one can stand before you" (Ez. 9:15). Or as the psalmist cries out, "If You mark iniquities, Adonai Yahweh, who stands?" (Ps. 130:3) NYLT). As King David implores in Psalm 143:2, "Do not bring Your servant into judgment, for no one living is righteous before You" (NIV84).

And when the day of God's wrath comes (2 Thess. 1:6-10), the Bible declares in Revelation, chapter 6:

> [15] And the kings of the earth, and the great men, and the rich, and the chiefs of thousands, and the mighty, and every slave, and every freeman, hid themselves in the dens, and in the rocks of the mountains, [16] and they say to the mountains and to the rocks, "Fall upon us, and hide us from the face of Him who is sitting upon the throne, and from the anger of the Lamb! [17] Because the great day of His anger did come, and who is able to stand?"

(Rev. 6:15-17 NYLT)

There is no where to escape God's wrath. Hell has no exists. As Dante fictitiously but hauntingly depicted in his book *Inferno*,

> "Through me is the way to the city of woe,
> Through me is the way to eternal pain,
> Through me is the way to a lost people.
> Justice moved my great Creator
> Divine Power made me,
> the Supreme Wisdom and the Primal Love.
> Before me, nothing else was created
> nothing, but the eternal and I last eternally.
> Abandon all hope, you who enter here."

Therefore, men everywhere should be frantic with desperation to know with absolute certainty how they can possibly be justified by God. They should cry out with Job, "is there no mediator [or arbitrator] between" (Job 9:33) God and myself?! As Eli the priest admonished his sons "if a man sin against a man, then God has judged him; but if a man sin against Yahweh, who prays for him?" (1 Sam. 2:25 NYLT). The whole human race is in desperate need of an Mediator, and Arbitrator, an Intercessor to propitiate the wrath of God's holy indignation and just condemnation.

The term *propitiation* refers literally to the mercy seat of the Old Testament—the lid of the ark of the covenant upon which, on every tenth day of the seventh month, the blood of the vicarious lamb was sprinkled to atone for the sins of the people. It means to appease or placate the wrath of God by taking away the sin of the sinner. All men everywhere need a Reconciler to bring them back to God

(2 Cor. 5:18-20) by propitiating, appeasing, or placating His righteous anger.

In Romans, chapter 3, we read:

> 21 And now apart from law the righteousness of God has been manifested, testified to by the Law and the Prophets, 22 and the righteousness of God, through faith in Jesus Christ, to all and upon all those believing. For there is no difference—23 for all did sin, and are come short of the glory of God, 24 being declared righteous freely by His grace through the redemption that is in Christ Jesus, 25 whom God did set forth as a propitiation by His blood, through faith, for the showing forth of His righteousness, because of the passing over of the bygone sins in the forbearance of God, 26 for the showing forth of His righteousness in the present time, that He might be both righteous and declare as righteous he who has faith in Jesus.
>
> (Rom. 3:21-26 NYLT)

Jesus Christ is that Reconciler, Mediator, Arbitrator, and Intercessor who propitiated—by His blood as the pure and spotless Lamb of God—God's righteous wrath. As verse 25 of this passage declares, God set forth His one and only Son as the Propitiator for all who believe. We see this also in the prayer of the early church in Acts, chapter 4, beginning with verse 27:

> 27 For gathered together—truthfully—against Your holy Servant Jesus, whom You did anoint, were both Herod and Pontius Pilate,

with ethnic groups and peoples of Israel, [28] to do whatever Your hand and Your counsel did determine beforehand to come to pass.

(Acts 4:27-28 NYLT)

In 2 Corinthians, the Apostle Paul writes, "Now all things are of God, who has reconciled us to Himself through Christ Jesus..." (2 Cor. 5:18). Jesus Himself declared, "For 'God so loved the world, that He gave His only begotten Son, that whosoever believes in Him should not perish but have everlasting life." (Jn. 3:16).

In Isaiah 53—often called the Fifth Gospel—we find Isaiah prophesying 700 years before Christ:

[3] "He is despised, and discarded of men,
A man of pains, and acquainted with suffering,
And as one hiding the face from us, He is despised, and we esteemed Him not.
[4] Surely our sicknesses he has borne,
And our pains—He has carried them,
And we—we have esteemed Him plagued, smitten of God, and afflicted.
[5] And He is pierced for our transgressions,
Bruised for our iniquities,
The chastisement of our peace is on Him,
And by his bruise there is healing to us.
[6] All of us like sheep have wandered,
Each to his own way we have turned,
And Yahweh has laid on Him the punishment of us all.
[7] He was oppressed and He was afflicted,
Yet He opens not his mouth,
As a lamb to the slaughter He is brought,
And as a sheep before its shearers is dumb,

So He opens not his mouth.

8 By restraint and by judgment He has been taken,

And of His generation who meditates—

That He has been cut off from the land of the living?

By the transgression of My people He is plagued.

9 And His grave is appointed with the wicked,

And with the rich at His death,

Because He has done no violence,

Nor is deceit in His mouth.

10 And Yahweh has delighted to bruise Him,

He has made Him suffer,

If His soul makes an offering for guilt,

He sees His seed -- He prolongs His days,

And the pleasure of Yahweh prospers in His hand.

11 Of the labor of His soul He sees—and is satisfied,

Through His knowledge the righteous One, My Servant, gives righteousness to many,

And their iniquities He bears.

12 Therefore I give a portion to Him among the great,

And He apportions spoil with the mighty,

Because He exposed His soul to death,

And with transgressors He was numbered,

And the sin of many He has borne,

And for transgressors He intercedes."

(Is. 53:3-12 NYLT)

Catch the legal transaction that Isaiah describes here:

- **Verses 4-5:** God the Son was stricken, smitten, afflicted, wounded, bruised, and chastised (or punished) for our sins in our place.
- **Verse 6:** God the Father has laid on His Son the iniquity or sin of us all.
- **Verse 8:** Again, Christ was stricken, or bore the penalty, of the sin of His people.
- **Verse 10:** God the Father bruised His Son and grieved Him in order to make Him a sin offering.
- **Verse 11:** Christ will justify many by bearing their iniquities (or sins).
- **Verse 12:** Christ, by bearing our sins, has become our Intercessor before God.

In other words, Jesus Christ is our sole Reconciler, Mediator, Arbitrator, and Intercessor who—by His blood on the hill called Calvary—propitiated or appeased the wrath of God. Consequently, it is only through this pure and spotless Lamb of God that we are justified before God. Our English word *justification* comes from the Greek word *dikaios*, which literally means to be declared righteous. It is a legal verdict in which God declares that we are righteous through an act of double imputation.

Double imputation is the Biblical doctrine that tries to explain the legal transaction that took place at Calvary. The first imputation is that our sin was imputed—or conveyed or transferred—to Christ who drank our hell for us, and the second imputation is that His righteousness was imputed to us by which we experience eternal life. In 2 Corinthians, chapter 5, we read:

> [17] So that if anyone is in Messiah, he is a new creature: the old things did pass away, behold! —all things have become new! [18] And all

things are of God, who reconciled us to Himself through Jesus Messiah, and did give to us the deaconing of reconciliation — [19] that God was in Messiah reconciling the world to Himself, not imputing to them their trespasses; and having put in us the word of the reconciliation.

[20] We, therefore, are ambassadors on Messiah's behalf, as if God were calling through us, we implore you on Messiah's behalf, "Be reconciled to God." [21] For Him who did not know sin, He made sin on our behalf, that we may become the righteousness of God in Him.

(2 Cor. 5:17-21 NYLT)

Let me highlight a couple of things from this passage:

• **Verse 19:** Christ reconciles His elect children to Himself by not imputing — or conveying or transferring — their sins to them.

• **Verse 21:** Christ, who was not a sinner, was treated as though He were, so that we, who most definitely are sinners, might be treated as though we were not. As John Piper has explained this verse, "Christ bore an alien sin and suffered for it, that we might bear an alien righteousness and live through it." In short, Christ's righteousness has become our righteousness!

And we see this demonstrated throughout Scripture. 1 Corinthians 1:30, for instance, declares, "But of Him [i.e., God] you are in Christ Jesus, who became for us wisdom from God, and righteousness and sanctification and redemption." Romans 5:19 reads, "For just as one man's

[Adam's] disobedience many were made sinners, so also by one Man's [Christ's] obedience many will be made righteous." Or as Romans 10:4 tells us, "For Christ is the end of the law for righteousness, to everyone who believes." Finally, the Apostle Paul declares in the third chapter of Philippians, beginning with verse 7:

> 7 But what things were to me gains, these I have counted, because of Messiah, loss. 8 Yes, indeed, and I count all things to be loss, because of the excellency of the knowledge of Messiah Jesus my Lord, because of whom I suffered the loss of all things, and do count them to be dung, that I may gain Messiah, 9 and be found in Him, not having my own righteousness, which is of the law, but that which is through faith in Christ—the righteousness that is from God by faith.
>
> (Phil. 3:7-9 NYLT)

This is what Biblical justification is—a past-tense, completed legal verdict that took place outside of ourselves upon a hill called Calvary. Justification is a forensic or legal declaration or verdict that we are as righteous as Christ is righteous in the sight of God. In Christ, all of our sin—past, present, and future, is nailed to the cross and we bear it no more!

In Christ, your righteousness is not found in yourself but in heaven, seated at the right hand of God the Father where He even now is reigning. Your righteousness is not dependent upon your own weak and fallible self, but rather it is secure and guaranteed by Him who is the same yesterday, today, and forever. Your righteousness doesn't waiver when your faith waivers. Nor does it get stronger when your faith gets stronger. Your past failures do not affect your righteousness. Your current temptations do not affect your righteousness. Your present circumstances do not affect your righteousness. Rather, your righteousness is perfect as Christ is perfect, for Christ's performance— not your performance—is your righteousness.

2. **Appropriated by Faith.**

Now that we know what justification is, the second question we must ask ourselves is how do we make this justification—this double imputation of our sin for Christ's righteousness—ours? Christ's death is a historical fact. Our redemption through His perfect life and sacrificial blood is a done deal. Our justification is a completed legal transaction paid in full 2,000 years ago. So how do we appropriate this abstract reality and make it our own? Or, to put it another way, what is the instrument or agency by which we are declared righteous in Christ? It is one thing to believe in a general, abstract way that Christ died for sinners, it is quite another to believe that Christ died specifically and particularly for me.

In Romans, chapter 4, we read:

> [16] Because of this it is of faith, that it may be according to grace, so the promise being sure to all the seed, not to those who are of the law only, but also to those who are of the faith of Abraham, who is the father of us all [17] (according as it has been written, "I have set you a father of many nations") before Him whom he did believe—God, who is quickening the dead, and is calling the things that be not as being; [18] who, against hope, in hope did believe, so that he is becoming the father of

many nations, according to what was spoken:
"So shall your seed be." ¹⁹ And having not
been weak in faith, he did not consider his
own body, already become dead (being about
a hundred years old) and the deadness of
Sarah's womb. ²⁰ And he did not stagger in
unbelief at the promise of God, but was
strengthened in faith, having given glory to
God, ²¹ and having been fully persuaded that
what He had promised He is also able to do,
²² wherefore also it was imputed to him for
righteousness. ²³ And it was not written for his
account alone, that it was imputed to him,
²⁴ but also for ours, to whom it is about to be
imputed—to us believing on Him who raised
up Jesus our Lord out of the dead, ²⁵ who was
delivered up because of our offenses, and was
raised up because of our being declared
righteous.

(Rom. 4:16-25 NYLT)

Notice the correlation that the Apostle Paul paints for
us. In verse 22 he concludes that Abraham—by the simple
instrumentality or agency of faith in believing God's
promises—was imputed as righteousness. Actually, the
word *imputed* used here comes from the Greek word
logizomai, which means to compute (i.e., take into
account), reckon (i.e., come to a bottom line), or reason to
a logical conclusion. It is often translated in our various
English translations as *imputed, credited, numbered*, or
accounted. So in verse 22 Paul tells us that Abraham
believed God and was therefore imputed—or accounted,
reckoned, or credited—with an alien righteousness not his
own, and in verse 24 he explains that in the same way we

who believe in God's free gift of justification through Christ will also be imputed—or accounted, reckoned, or credited —with an alien—that is, Christ's—righteousness.

And then Paul concludes in the very next verse— Romans 5:1— that, "Therefore, having been justified by faith, we have peace with God through our Lord Jesus Christ." Justification—being declared righteous by God—is by the simple instrumentality of faith.   Or as the Apostle writes in Romans 1:17: "For in it [i.e., the Gospel] the righteousness of God is revealed from faith to faith, as it is written, 'The just shall live by faith'" (quoting Hab. 2:4).   In Romans 3:22 Paul states that the righteousness of God is imputed "though faith in Jesus Christ to all and on all who believe."   As Jesus Himself makes this explicit in John 6:47, "'Most assuredly, I say to you, he who believes in Me has everlasting life.'"

3. *Sola Fide.*

The third question we must answer is whether faith excludes works, and the answer the Bible provides in verse after verse is that this justification is by faith and by faith alone. *Sola Fide!* It is not one of faith plus works, but of faith alone.   It is not one of faith plus keeping the law, but of faith alone.   It is not one of faith plus self-righteousness, but of faith alone. It is not one of faith plus merit, but one of faith alone.   Again, the only thing we contribute to our justification is our sin—our need to be justified in the first place.

We see this explained in the second and third stanza of the hymn *Rock of Ages*:

> 2 Not the labor of my hands
> Can fulfill Thy law's demands;
> Could my zeal no respite know,

Could my tears forever flow,
All could never sin erase,
Thou must save, and save by grace.

3 Nothing in my hands I bring,
Simply to Thy cross I cling;
Naked, come to Thee for dress,
Helpless, look to Thee for grace:
Foul, I to the fountain fly,
Wash me, Savior, or I die.

Justification is by grace alone through faith alone or there is no justification. Turn with me to Galatians, chapter 2, where beginning with verse 11 we read Paul describing another gospel preached by Judiazers (i.e., Jewish legalists) that even caused the Apostle Peter to stumble:

11 And when Peter came to Antioch, I stood up against him to the face, because he was blameworthy; 12 for before the coming of certain men from Jacob, he was eating with the ethnic groups, but when they came, he was withdrawing and separating himself, fearing those of the circumcision. 13 And also did the other Jews join him in stage-acting hypocrisy, so that also Barnabas was carried away by their stage-acting hypocrisy.
14 But when I saw that they are not walking uprightly to the truth of the gospel, I said to Peter before all, "If you, being a Jew, live in the manner of the ethnic groups, and not in the manner of the Jews, why do you compel the ethnic groups to Judaize? 15 We, by nature Jews and not sinners of the ethnic

groups, [16] having known also that a man is not declared righteous by works of law but through faith in Jesus Messiah—even we who did believe in Messiah Jesus—that we might be declared righteous by faith in Messiah and not by works of law; for by works of the law shall no flesh be declared righteous."

(Gal. 2:11-16 NYLT)

These Judiazers were professing Jewish believers in Jesus Christ who traveled to Antioch from Jerusalem. But the "gospel" they professed was one of faith plus works. Namely, they taught that one must not only have faith, but that one must also perfectly keep all of the Jewish ceremonial and religious laws—laws mandating circumcision of male children on the eight day, separation from Gentles (even Gentile believers), keeping certain holy days, and maintaining a Kosher diet. But Paul boldly confronted this false gospel, declaring in verse 16 that:

[16] having known also that a man is not declared righteous by works of law but through faith in Jesus Messiah—even we who did believe in Messiah Jesus—that we might be declared righteous by faith in Messiah and not by works of law; for by works of the law shall no flesh be declared righteous."

(Gal. 2:16 NYLT)

This is the heart, the essence, of the Gospel—justification by faith alone. Not of faith plus good works, but of faith alone. Notice in this passage how Paul describes the purpose of the law. In verse 13 that it is to show us that we are self-righteous hypocrites unable to

61

keep the law. He says this again in verse 15 when he calls out Peter and these Judiazer legalists—who themselves lived like the heathen Gentiles because they were unable to keep the law—as hypocrites for compelling Gentile believers to keep a law that they themselves could not keep.

According to Galatians 3:21, the purpose of the law is not to give life through perfect obedience. Rather, the purpose of the law was to show us that we cannot perfectly obey the law and, consequently, that we cannot be justified by the law. We read in Galatians, chapter 3:

> 22 But the Holy Writing did shut up together all under sin, that the promise by faith in Jesus Messiah may be given to those believing. 23 And before the coming of faith, we were kept under law, we were being kept, shut up to the faith about to be revealed. 24 Therefore, the law became our guardian unto Christ, that by faith we may be declared righteous. 25 But the faith having come, we are no more under a guardian.
>
> (Gal. 3:22-25 NYLT)

Verse 22 explains the purpose of the law—that all mankind everywhere might be condemned as sinners who cannot save themselves, irregardless of how much merit, work, and righteousness they might earn. Again, in verse 24 Paul describes the law as our guardian or tutor to bring us to Christ. How does it tutor us? By stripping us of any sense of self-righteousness so that we might trust completely Christ's perfect, final, and sufficient atonement for our sins.

In Romans, chapter 3, we read:

> 19 And we have known that as many things as the law says, it says to those under the law, that every mouth may be stopped, and all the world may come under judgment before God. 20 Therefore by works of the law shall no flesh be declared righteous before Him, for by the law is the knowledge of sin.
>
> (Rom. 3:19-20 NYLT)

Here in verse 19 Paul again describes the purpose of the law—to stop every mouth as all mankind everywhere realizes their guilt before a holy and righteous Judge. Then, in verse 20 Paul again describes the law as a tutor who teaches us that we are sinful and in desperate need to be made unsinful so that we might be reconciled and at peace with a just and perfect God. Good works, legalism, New Year's resolutions, and any other kind of human effort only shows us that we will never get to heaven on our own power. Law keeping only serves to show us that we are sinners who love our sin and cannot do anything but sin and therefore we need a perfect Redeemer to give us His alien righteousness.

And this justification through Christ—by which we are imputed with His righteousness and therefore declared righteous before God—is a gift that we can only appropriate and make our own by faith and faith alone. We see this in Romans, chapter 4:

> 4 And to him who is working, the recompense is not imputed by grace but of debt. 5 And to him who is not working but is believing upon Him who is declaring righteous the impious, his faith is imputed for righteousness, 6 even

as David also speaks of the blessedness of the man to whom God imputes righteousness apart from works:

7 `"Blessed are they whose lawless acts were forgiven,

And whose sins were covered;

8 Blessed is the man to whom the LORD shall not impute sin."

(Rom. 4:4-8 NYLT)

Notice that Paul again here describes the double imputation that occurs at the moment of justification. Verses 5-6: we are imputed with an alien righteousness not our own that we might live through it. And in verses 7-8: our sins are imputed to the perfect sinless Lamb of God so that He might experience hell as our substitute in our place. And in verse 5 Paul states that this double imputation by which we are justified is only available through faith alone because, as verse 4 warns us, if we try to add works to our faith we actually nullify our faith and we are back to owing God a debt of unrighteousness that we could never work off.

Justification, therefore, is either by faith alone or it is by works alone, for Scripture emphatically and explicitly denies the possibility that it can be achieve by both. We see this again in Romans 11:6, where Paul writes, "And if [justification is] by grace, then it is no longer of works; otherwise grace is no longer grace. But if it is of works, it is no longer grace; otherwise work is no longer work."

Justification is by grace alone through faith alone to the exclusion of being—in whole or in part—supplemented or added to by works.

4. Faith is a Gracious Gift.

The fourth and final question we must ask is whether this faith by which alone we are justified is in fact our work or a gift from God. Do we muster it up out of our own will power, or is it a completely unearned gift from outside of ourselves? In Matthew, chapter 16, we read:

> 13 And Jesus, having come to the parts of Caesarea Philippi, was asking His disciples, saying, "Who do men say that I, the Son of Man, am?"
>
> 14 And they said, "Some say John the Baptist, others Elijah, and others Jeremiah or one of the prophets."
>
> 15 He said to them, "And you—who do you say that I am?"
>
> 16 And Simon Peter answering said, "You are the Messiah, the Son of the living God."
>
> 17 And Jesus answering said to him, "Blessed are you, Simon Bar-Jonah, because flesh and blood did not reveal this to you, but My Father who is in the heavens."
>
> (Matt. 16:13-17 NYLT)

There is no room for boasting on Judgment Day that you were smart enough to figure this whole justification thing out on your own. There is no room for pride that you mustered up enough faith to believe the Gospel message. No, in this passage Jesus explicitly excludes boasting, telling His disciples that they only believed because His Father graciously enabled them to.

We see this in numerous other passages in Scripture. For instance, Peter writes, "To those who have obtained like precious faith with us by the righteousness of our God and Savior Jesus Christ" (2 Pet. 1:2). Peter's audience obtained their faith. They did not earn it. They did not work for it. They did not merit it in any way. It was not of themselves but given to them. That's what obtain means. And they obtained it as a gift purchased by the righteous life and death of Jesus Christ.

Similarly, Paul writes that, "...to you it has been granted on behalf of Christ, not only to believe in Him, but also to suffer for His sake" (Phil. 1:29). You do not have to be granted something that is yours. You do not have to be granted to do something that you are already perfectly capable of doing. For instance, you would not say that I granted you breakfast this morning because I had nothing whatsoever to do with your breakfast this morning. You did. But you would say that if I had everything to do with your breakfast this morning. Similarly, God grants us faith because we have nothing to do with it.

Peter makes this explicit in his sermon recorded in Acts 3, stating that, "...faith [] comes through Him [Jesus Christ]" (Acts 3:16). Not merely faith in Jesus Christ, which Peter does state earlier in verse 16. But that the faith to believe in Jesus Christ comes from Jesus Christ. It does not come for human will, effort, or contribution, but as a gracious, unearned gift from God and God alone.

We find Paul echoes this point in Ephesians 2:

> 8 For by grace you have been saved through faith. And this is not of your doing; it is the gift of God, 9 not of works, lest anyone should boast.
>
> (Eph. 2:8-9 ESV)

Verse 8 makes explicit that you are saved by grace through faith, and that this faith is not of your own doing but is the gift of God. And verse 9 tells us the reason or the purpose for *Sola Fide*: so that no one should boast before God. Or as Paul put it in Romans, chapter 4:

> [27] Where, then, is boasting? It is excluded. On what principle? On that of observing the law? No, but on that of faith. [28] For we maintain that a man is justified by faith apart from observing the law.
>
> (Rom. 4:27-28 NIV84)

Justification, therefore, is by grace alone through faith alone so that God alone gets all the glory. Justification is, from start to finish, an act of God's unearned, unmerited favor. He initiated it. He implemented it. He obtained it. He applies it. He guarantees it. And He will complete it until the very end. All, as Ephesians 1:14 tells us, to the praise of His glory and His glory alone.

Concluding Implications:

In conclusion, justification by grace alone through faith alone is the Gospel; without it there is no Good News. There are, tragically, many professing Christians who believe that justification is only by faith plus good works. That, yes, faith is important. Even that it may be necessary, essential, and foundational. But that we have to then somehow earn or merit this free gift of God. It is so incredibly hard for man to accept *Sola Fide* because it means abandoning any confidence or hope in his own self-righteousness. His own self-sufficiency. His own merit and goodness.

But we can never, ever, become righteous enough for God, either in this life or in an intermediate place of purging called Purgatory in the next life. Each of our immeasurable sins against an infinite God demands infinite satisfaction in hell. Or, to put it another way, just one teeny-tiny, "white" sin must be punished with an eternity in hell. The punishment for a thousand such sins, therefore, is a thousand infinities. But each of us have sinned far more than a thousand teeny-tiny "white" sins. Rather, our sins are as numerous as the stars in the heavens or the sand on the sea shore, so our just sentence before a holy and righteous God is one of an uncountable infinities in hell.

This is a debt that we can never hope to erase. But it gets even worse than that, for we never stop adding to it because we cannot stop sinning. The apostate Roman Catholic Church believe in justification by faith, but not by faith alone. They believe in faith plus good works, and that if at the time of your death you have not earned enough merit to become righteous in your own right before God, you must be purged of your sin in Purgatory. But the problem with this heresy is that the sinner doesn't stop sinning in Purgatory, and with each trillisecond that passes he continues to sin and thereby continues to incur never-ending infinities in hell that he must now also purge himself of. It is a treadmill of sin and damnation that he can never get off of. And even if somehow he could purge himself of his sin and make himself righteous enough for heaven, his pride over doing so would condemn him once again to hell.

In closing, let us look at the Apostle Paul's denunciation of the so-called "Gospel" of the Judiazing legalists in the strongest terms possible:

> 6 I marvel that you are so quickly removed from Him who did call you in the grace of Messiah to another gospel; 7 which is not another, but there be certain who are troubling you and desire to pervert the gospel of the

Messiah; 8 But even if we or a messenger out of heaven herald to you a gospel different from the gospel we did herald to you—anathema let him be! 9 As we have said before, and now say again, If anyone may herald to you a gospel different from what you did receive—anathema let him be! 10 For do I now persuade men, or God? Or do I seek to please men? For if yet I still please men, Christ's slave I cannot be.

(Gal. 1:6-10 NYLT)

There is no other Gospel than justification by grace alone through faith alone. It is not good news to offer men faith plus good works, for such good news only leads to a life of hypocrisy and an eternal death in hell. Nor is it good news because it mocks Christ's death. As Paul put it in Galatians 2:21, "if righteousness comes through the law, then Christ died in vain." If you seek to add to or supplement Christ's atoning sacrifice with your good works and righteousness, you are, in effect, saying to God that Christ's atonement is insufficient. That His life of perfect obedience to the law of God was, in fact, imperfect and insufficient. That His death upon the cross in which He experienced hell for your sin was imperfect and insufficient.

And that's arrogant blasphemy. You plus Christ is, in reality, you without Christ. And you without Christ is you dead in your trespasses and sins with no hope other than eternal damnation. In short, there can be no other good news than *Sola Fide* because Christ alone—apart from you —is more than sufficient to save, now and forever. As the author of Hebrews proclaims—Christ Jesus offered HImself once for all as the all-sufficient sacrifice for sins for all time and now He reigns forevermore at the right hand of God the Father (Heb. 1:3, 7:27, 10:12)! Praise the Lord!

4 SOLA FIDE (PART 2)

*I*n the last chapter we begun our study of the doctrine of *Sola Fide*—that justification is by grace alone through faith alone. This free gift—in which our sin is imputed to Christ and He experienced hell for it and His righteousness is imputed to us and we live eternally through it—is appropriated by the instrument or agency of faith. And it is by faith alone to the exclusion of works, for the two are mutually incompatible. It is either 100% faith or 100% works. And this faith by which we are saved is not something that we mustered up but is solely a gracious gift from God so that no man may boast in His presence.

I.   Impostor Faith.   We established, therefore, that justification is by faith and faith alone. But this means nothing unless and until we also define what faith is. It is no good telling people that they need faith in order to be forgiven and at peace and reconciled with a holy and righteous God if we don't also tell them what it means to have faith. And so beginning in this chapter we are going to examine the vital and essential question of what is saving faith.

I.A. Examples from John. The reason this question is so vital and essential is because it is not only possible, but also probable, that many have a false faith. An impostor trust. A nominal religion.   These impostors are CINOs: *C*hristians *i*n *N*ame *O*nly. And our churches are filled with them.   They have head knowledge, but no heart knowledge.   They know things *about* God, but they don't know God.   They may live moral lives, but they have not yet been birthed from above by the Holy Spirit into new creations (2 Cor. 5:17). They may be good people, but all their righteous acts remain as filthy as menstrual rages (Is. 64:6). They have deceived and deluded themselves into thinking that they have saving faith when in fact they don't have an ounce of saving faith whatsoever.

Let's look at a few examples just from the Gospel of John itself, beginning with John, chapter 2:

> [23] And as He was in Jerusalem at the Passover, during the feast many, beholding the signs that He was doing, believed in His name. [24] But Jesus Himself was not trusting Himself to them, because of His knowing all men, [25] and because He had no need that any should testify concerning man, for He Himself was knowing what was in man.
>
> (Jn. 2:23-25 NYLT)

In short, Jesus had no absolutely no confidence in their faith. None whatsoever. Why? Because verse 24 tells us that He knows us far better than we know ourselves and He knew that their faith was an impostor faith. And how was their faith defective? Because verse 23 tells us that they "believed in His name when they saw the signs which He did" (emphasis added). Some of them may have even believed that He was the long-promised Messiah, but they only believed because of the signs in order to see more signs. They believed in Him not as the spotless sacrificial Lamb of God, but as a wizard, a magician, who could not only meet their every need but deliver their nation from bondage under Rome rule. They had faith. Doubtless it was sincere and passionate. It was even in the right Person. But it was not saving faith.

Then in John, chapter 6, we read:

51 "I am the living bread that came down out of the heaven. If any one may eat of this bread he shall live—to the age; and the bread that I shall give is My flesh, which I will give for the life of the world."

52 The Jews, therefore, were striving with one another, saying, "How is this One able to give us His flesh to eat?"

53 Jesus, therefore, said to them, "Amen! Amen!—I say to you, unless you eat the flesh of the Son of Man, and unless you drink His blood, you have no life in yourselves. 54 He who is eating My flesh and is drinking My blood has life—to the age, and I will raise him up in the last day. 55 For My flesh truly is food, and My blood truly is drink. 56 He who is eating My flesh, and is drinking My blood, remains in me, and I in him. 57 According as the living Father sent me, and I live because of the Father, he also who is eating Me, even that one shall live because of Me. 58 This is the bread that came down out of the heaven— not as your fathers did eat the manna and died; he who is eating this bread shall live—to the age."

59 These things He said in a synagogue, teaching in Capernaum. 60 Many, therefore, of His disciples, having heard this, said, "This word is hard; who is able to hear it?"

61 And Jesus, having known in Himself that His disciples are murmuring about this, said to them, "Does this stumble you? 62 What then, if you may behold the Son of Man going up

where He was before? [63] The Spirit it is that is giving life; the flesh does not profit anything. The sayings that I speak to you are spirit, and they are life. [64] But there are certain of you who do not believe." For Jesus had known from the beginning who they are who are not believing, and who is he who will deliver him up. [65] And He said, "Because of this I have said to you —no one is able to come unto Me if it may not have been granted him from My Father." [66] From this time many of His disciples went away backward, and were no more walking with Him.

(Jn. 6:51-66 NYLT)

Jesus had many followers. Not just the Twelve Apostles, but many other disciples who would follow Him day after day as He preached throughout Palestine. And verse 2 of chapter 6 tells us that "a great multitude followed Him because they saw His signs which He performed on those who were diseased." And later in the chapter we are told that Jesus fed 5,000 of His followers from "five barley loaves and two small fish" (vs. 9). Then they followed Him across the Sea of Galilee (vs. 24-25) because, as Jesus tells us in verse 26, they ate of the loaves and were filled."

And in verse 27 He admonishes them not to "labor for the food which perishes, but for the food which endures to everlasting life, which the Son of Man will give you." He then explains to them in the passage that we just read that He is "the living bread which came down from heaven" (vs. 51). But many of His disciples rejected Him, being too full of the bread of this world. They turned their back on Him and, as verse 66 tells us, "walked with Him no more."

They had faith. Doubtless it was sincere and passionate. It was even in the right Person. But it was not saving faith.

Then in the next chapter, chapter 7, of John we read:

> 2 And the feast of the Jews was near—that of Tabernacles. 3 His brothers, therefore, said unto Him, "Remove from here and go away to Judea, that Your disciples also may behold Your works that You do." 4 For no one does anything in secret while he himself seeks to be in public. If You do these things, manifest Yourself to the world." 5 For not even His brothers were believing in Him.
>
> (Jn. 7:2-5 NYLT)

His brothers—who Mark 3:21 tells us had earlier thought Jesus was insane and needed to be committed to the funny farm—are here urging Him to go to Jerusalem for the big feast and on this international stage, in front of Jews from all over the ancient world, perform His miraculous signs. Perhaps they were even hoping that the Jewish crowds would then make Him king as He led the Jewish armies in victory again Rome. But John tells us that this belief was not real belief. Jesus' brothers had faith. Doubtless it was sincere and passionate. It was even in the right Person. But it was not saving faith.

Finally, let us look at John, chapter 12:

> 37 Yet He having done so many signs before them, they were not believing in Him...
> 42 Still, however, also out of the rulers many did believe in Him, but because of the Pharisees they were not confessing, that they might not be put out of the synagogue; 43 for

they loved the glory of men more than the glory of God.

(Jn. 12:37, 42-43 NYLT)

In verse 37 John tells us that many were hardened (vs. 40) to Who Jesus really was, despite all the miraculous signs He had performed among them. Nevertheless, John tells us in verse 42 that there were quite a few, even among the rulers, who privately professed to believe in Jesus. But later in verse 42 John tells us that they could not bring themselves to publicly acknowledge Jesus before men because, as verse 43 explains, "they loved the praise of men more than the praise of God." Their belief, such as it was, was shallow, skin deep, and full of fear; easily overpowered by their faith in men. They had faith. Doubtless it was sincere and passionate. It was even in the right Person. But it was not saving faith.

I.B. Narrow is the Way. None of these four examples should surprise us, for time after time Jesus warned against impostor faith masquerading as real faith. For instance, in Matthew 7 we read:

> [13] "Go in through the narrow gate, because wide is the gate, and broad the way that is leading to the destruction, and many are those going in through it. [14] How narrow is the gate and afflicted the way that is leading to the life, and few are those finding it!

(Matt. 7:13-14 NYLT)

Almost no one lives and dies thinking that they are going to hell. Rather, thousands die every single day thinking that they are going to heaven. That they have sufficiently appeased whatever deity they serve to punch their ticket to paradise. But Jesus tells us that a literal flood of humanity have entered through the wide gate unto the broad road that leads to destruction. They may have faith. It doubtless may be sincere and passionate faith. It may even be in the right Person of Jesus Christ. But it is not saving faith.

A few verses later, beginning with verse 21 of Matthew 7, we read:

> [21] "Not every one who is saying to Me, "Lord, Lord,' shall come into the kingdom of the heavens; but he who is doing the will of My Father who is in the heavens. [22] Many will say to Me in that day, 'Lord, Lord, have we not in You name prophesied? And in Your name cast out demons? And in Your name done many mighty things?' [23] And then I will confess to them that, 'I never knew you, depart from Me you who are working lawlessness.'"

> (Matt. 7:21-23 NYLT)

Jesus warns that on Judgement Day there will be many guilty souls standing before that Great White Throne who will protest that they really were believers. That they really were Christians. Look again at verse 22—they even call Christ "Lord" and, as evidence of their conversion, cite all the supernatural miracles they thought they had done in His name. But all they will hear in reply are the awful words: "I never knew you; depart from Me, you who practice lawlessness!" (vs. 23). These professing believers may have faith. It doubtless may be sincere and passionate faith. It may even be in the right Person of Jesus Christ. But it is not saving faith.

Then a few chapters later in Matthew 13 we read:

> 1 And in that day Jesus, having gone forth from the house, was sitting by the sea. 2 And many multitudes were gathered together unto Him, so that He, having gone into a boat, sat down, and all the multitude stood on the beach. 3 And He spoke to them many things in similes, saying: "Behold!—the sower went forth to sow. 4 And in his sowing, some indeed fell by the wayside, and the birds did come and devour them. 5 And others fell upon the rocky places where they did not have much earth, and immediately they sprang forth because they had no depth of earth. 6 And the sun—having risen—they were scorched, and because they had no root they withered. 7 And others fell upon the thorns, and the thorns did come up and choke them. 8 And others fell upon the good ground and were giving fruit, some indeed a hundredfold, and some sixty, and some thirty. 9 He who is having ears to hear, let him hear!"...
>
> 18 "You, therefore, hear you the simile of the sower: 19 Everyone hearing the word of the kingdom and is not understanding, the evil one comes and catches that which has been sown in his heart. This is that which was sown by the wayside. 20 And that sown on the rocky places, this is he who is hearing the word and immediately is receiving it with joy; 21 and he

has no root in himself, but is temporary. And persecution or tribulation having happened because of the word, immediately he is stumbled. [22] And that sown toward the thorns, this is he who is hearing the word, and the anxiety of this age, and the deceitfulness of riches, choke the word, and it becomes unfruitful. [23] And that sown on the good ground, this is he who is hearing the word and is understanding, who indeed bears fruit and makes: some indeed a hundredfold, and some sixty, and some thirty."

(Matt. 13:1-9, 18-23 NYLT)

Many start well (Gal. 5:7). Many may have responded to the Gospel invitation in a church service. Many may have gone to the altar and said a so-called "sinner's prayer." Many may make a public declaration of faith and have been baptized. Many may be active in their church and, to all appearances, appear to be sheep. Appear to be the real thing. Appear to be authentic Christians. But their faith is not persevering because it is not genuine. It is only skin deep and the charade is easily cast off in the face of Satanic deception, tribulation and persecution, and the cares of this world and the deceitfulness of riches. These professing believers may have faith. It doubtless may be sincere and passionate faith. It may even be in the right Person of Jesus Christ. But it is not saving faith.

I.C. Types of Impostors. So what are some examples of this type of fake response to the Gospel call?

The **first** type of impostor is one who thinks of Christ as their pimp daddy or enabler who will give them their best life now. That's what Judas thought. He saw Christ as an earthly king who was soon to establish His kingdom in which Judas would gain wealth and power. Others turn to Christ as a means of getting out of financial trouble, or trouble with the criminal court system, or trouble with their marriages, or trouble at school, or trouble with drugs and alcohol. They simply see Christ as a twelve-step program to becoming a better you.

They have bought hook, line, and sinker the lie told by Prosperity Gospel preachers that God will make them rich, healthy, and carefree if they just claim it and name it with enough faith in prayer. This is a poisonous, blasphemous, idolatrous lie that conveniently overlooks that Christ assures His elect that in this world they will have many tribulations (Jn. 16:33; see also Matt. 10:24-25, 24:9; Jn. 15:18-21, 16:3), and Paul tells us that it is only through such trials that we must enter the kingdom of God (Acts 14:22; see also 1 Pet. 4:12).

The **second** type of impostor is one who simply embraces Christ as their ticket to heaven, but nothing more. They don't echo with the Apostle Paul that, "for me to live is Christ, and to die is gain" (Phil. 1:21) because he wants to be with Christ forever. Rather, they simply want a carefree eternity; a ceaseless paradise. An endless party with family and friends in which they get to live out their most selfish imaginations for all eternity. They don't want heaven because Christ is there and, if they were honest, they would prefer He not be there because He would not approve of their definition of fun. They don't want to feast their souls on the infinite Christ, but rather indulge their sinful lusts upon infinite self-idolatry.

The **third** type of impostor is the one who embraces Christ as their ticket out of hell, but nothing more. They have come under just enough conviction of sin to know they are not at peace with God and, consequently, in danger of hell fire upon drawing their last breath. But they don't hate their sins so much as they don't want to go to hell. And in actuality, they would still want their sins if they could still escape hell.

Their conviction of sin is not that of godly sorrow over the fact that it blasphemies God, denigrates Him, and grieves His glory. They don't hate sin because they love God and do not want to offend His holiness, but only because they got caught. They don't hate their sin because God hates it, but because they don't want to go to hell.

And they don't hate their sin because it held Christ upon the cross of Calvary. That they were the ones who cried out to Pontius Pilate, "Crucify Him! Crucify Him!" That they were the ones who scourged Him ruthlessly with a Cat of Nine Tails. That they were the ones who mockingly shoved a crown of thorns upon His head, beat Him, and ridiculed Him. That they were the ones who drove the nails into His wrists and feet. That they were the ones who blasphemed Him and denied His deity. Rather, their conviction of sin is merely that of worldly sorrow—that of a criminal sorry that he got caught but who would do it again in a heartbeat if he thought he could get away with it.

The **fourth** type of impostor is the one who embraces Christ, but not Christ alone. Instead, they remains convinced that they must have Christ plus good works. Christ plus resolutions to become a better you. They want Christ while clinging to some resemblance of their self-righteousness. They think that they must make themselves good enough so that Christ will then come into their hearts. Or they think that Christ plus good works will be enough to outweigh their bad deeds and get them into heaven. Christ's blood and righteousness alone is not their sole hope of salvation, but Christ plus their own righteousness.

To use an analogy—let's pretend they owe the federal government $1 million in back taxes. But then their rich uncle steps in and gives them a $1 million check as a gift to completely wipe out their debt in its entirety. But these poor, deluded fools either think they have to become good enough to receive such a gift, or they think that the gift itself is insufficient on its own. They think it will only cover 80% of their debt and that they still have to come up with the remaining 20% on their own.

The **fifth** and **final** type of impostor is the one who sees something attractive about Christ but simply goes through the motions. They may be able to recite the creeds and confessions of the faith by heart. They may be able to answer both the long and the short catechisms. They may have memorized hundreds of Bible verses in AWANA.

They may have attended church from the moment they were born, going every time the church doors were open. They may have been the children of pastors or missionaries. They may have been baptized, whether as an infant or even as an adult professing faith in Christ. They may regularly partake of the Lord's Supper. They may give 20% of their money to the church, and another 20% to missions and charity.

They may be very sincere and heartfelt in their Christian walk. They may be part of the praise team, or youth leaders, or Sunday School teachers. They may be elders or deacons. They may be seminary professors or authors of Christian bestsellers. They may serve the law of God (Rom. 7:25), call it spiritual (vs. 14), and delight in it (vs. 22). They may perform miracles such as healing the sick and casting out demons (Matt. 7:22). They may even be willing to be martyred for the sake of Christ (1 Cor. 13:3).

But they have no life. They have head belief, not heart belief. They have an intellectual agreement, but no spiritual reality. They have Christ in name only, but no Christ within or Christ without. They remain spiritually dead with no life of Christ within them. "[T]hey have a zeal for God, but not according to [a living, personal (Jn. 17:3)] knowledge" (Rom. 10:2). Their faith was stillborn, never having been quickened by the Holy Spirit in the first place.

They have no bedrock seed of assurance, peace, and joy of their salvation. They believe with all their heart that Christ died for sinners, but not necessarily that Christ died for them. Instead, they place their trust in emotional experiences. In decisions made once upon a time. In a sinner's prayer they once recited. In a baptism they once had. In Hail Mary's once given. In their outstanding moral character. In their service to the Church. In intellectual understanding. They are content with the outward trappings of Christ without actually having Christ Himself. They are in love with an idea, a philosophy, a way of life, but not a Person. Their god is their morality, not Christ. It is their life at work in them, not His.

They are like the Pharisee in Luke 18 who thanked God that he was not like the tax collector next to him because, "'I fast twice a week [and] I give tithes of all that I possess'" (Lk. 18:12). Look at what their defense is as they stand before the Judgement Seat of Christ—"But Lord, look at what we did!" (Matt. 7:22). It is not one of, "we are unprofitable servants (Lk. 17:10) who could do nothing apart from You!" (Jn. 15:5). It is not one of having loved much because they were forgiven much (Lk. 7:36-50). It is not one of, "we were dead but Your Spirit has given us life in You!" Rather, these imitators are thrust out of the Kingdom of God because they "trusted in themselves[,] that they were righteous" (Lk. 18:9).

II. Essential Components of Saving Faith. So all this still begs the question of what is saving faith? We have established that there is such a thing as impostor faith, that Christ warns us against it, and that there can be at least five kinds of impostor faith. But what is real, genuine, authentic saving faith? In the rest of this chapter and those that follow we will examine several essential components or elements of saving faith. If any of these elements are not present, there is no saving faith. With that said, however, a believer, especially a young believer, may not be able to verbalize, much less understand, all these elements.

Nor will all of these elements be manifested to the same degree. For instance, some may come to saving faith after months, if not years, of soul-agonizing conviction of sin and guilt, while others do so with, comparatively, little godly sorrow. But real, genuine, authentic repentance is present in both individuals and will immediately, necessarily, and inevitably bear fruit.

Furthermore, some of these elements, though essential to saving faith, may actually occur, at least in part, before saving faith. For instance, an individual may experience some measure of repentance years before his actual conversion. Both Martin Luther and John Bunyan, for example, labored for years in hatred of, and repentance for, their sins. However, until a man is regenerated by the Holy Spirit, such repentance remains half-baked. Such individuals may even hate their sin because they fear offending a holy God; they may even seek to flee from their sin because they do not want to belittle the sacrifice of Christ upon Calvary; but because their repentance is not out of love for God it can never arise to godly sorrow leading to eternal life.

Or, to use another example, there are certain things that one must know or believe intellectually in order to exercise saving faith. Such intellectual consent, called in Latin *notitia* by the early Reformation Fathers, can occur months if not years before actual regeneration. Again, Martin Luther and John Bunyan had such intellectual knowledge long before they savingly received such knowledge. We often see this today when an individual is struggling to leave a religion, such as Mormonism or Islam, for Christ. They may accept as true the entire Gospel story and may even have better theology than you or I long before their heart follows their mind. A person may believe to be true the ancient creeds and confession of the Church, they may even be seminary professors or Bible school teachers, but such knowledge saves them not.

II.A.   Notitia.   But this brings us to the first essential component of saving faith—*notitia*.   The intellectual knowledge absolutely essential in order to someone to be saved.

The **first** thing that must be intellectually accepted is that there is only one true and living God who is holy and righteous, just and good. In Hebrews, chapter 11, we read:

> [1] Now faith is the title-deed of things hoped for, the proof of matters not seen. [2] For by this the elders obtained a good testimony. [3] By faith we understand the ages to have been prepared by a saying of God, in regard to the things seen not having come out of things appearing...[6] But apart from faith it is impossible to please well, for it behoves him

who is coming to God to believe that He is, and to those earnestly seeking Him He becomes a paymaster.

(Heb. 11:1-3, 6 NYLT)

In order to be saved, we have to accept and receive with our minds that God is real. That He exists. That the God of the Bible is the only true and living God. That He is the creator of everything that is, was, and is to come. That He is our Maker and Master. That we were created for His glory.

We must also know that we must not have any other gods before Him nor make any carved images or idols and worship them (Ex. 20:3-4), for He alone is worthy of all of our love, worship, adoration, and fear. That all other gods and religions are lies and false. That we cannot be a Buddhist and a Christian at the same time. Or a Jehovah Witness and a Christian at the same time. Or a follower of our Native religion and a Christian at the same time.

Furthermore, we must know something of His character, as Yahweh proclaimed to Moses on Mount Sinai in Exodus 34:

> 5 And Yahweh comes down in a cloud, and stations Himself with him there, and calls in the Name of Yahweh. 6 And Yahweh passes over before his face, and calls: "Yahweh, Yahweh God, merciful and gracious, slow to anger, and abundant in kindness and truth, 7 keeping kindness for thousands, taking away iniquity and transgression and sin, and not entirely acquitting..."

(Ex. 34:5-7 NYLT)

The **second** thing that must be intellectually accepted in order to be saved is that one needs to believe that not only is God true, but His Word is also true. In other words, in order to exercise saving faith one must believe that God is trustworthy. That He has revealed Himself through a book called the Bible that exclusively reveals all things necessary for our salvation. That when the Bible speaks God speaks, and therefore it is to be believed, as God's instruction, in all that it affirms; obeyed, as God's command, in all that it requires; and embraced, as God's pledge, in all that it promises. That the only true, pure, and undefiled religion is found in the Bible.

The **third** thing that must be intellectually accepted in order to be saved is that one is a sinner who has fallen short of the glory of God (Rom. 3:23). That you are a God-hating rebel who hates God, loathes God, flees from God, and wants nothing to do with God. And that therefore you are under God's just condemnation and holy wrath with the sentence of eternal hell hanging over your head.

In order to be saved, you have to accept and receive with your mind that you are a sinner who cannot save yourself but are in desperate need of a Savior. You have to acknowledge that all your righteous acts are as menstrual rags (Is. 64:6). That you, like sheep, have gone astray, each one to his own way. That your heart is evil continually. That there is no one good but God alone. That God would be absolutely just if He sent you to hell this very moment.

That you cannot earn your salvation, and that you cannot keep your salvation. That you have no self-righteousness before salvation, and you have no self-righteousness after salvation. That you are unable to reform yourself, make yourself good enough for God, or otherwise to earn your way to heaven. That the only way for you to be forgiven and at peace and reconciled with God is by His gracious mercy alone.

The **fourth** and **final** thing that must be intellectually accepted in order to be saved is that one may be saved from the wrath of God through Jesus Christ. You cannot believe that Jesus was merely a good man or a great teacher. Rather, you have to believe that He is both fully God and fully man. That He is God incarnate. That He has always and will always exist as God and that He humbled Himself to be born of a woman and take on our flesh and blood. You certainly do not have to even begin to understand how this hypostatic union is possible, you just have to believe that it is true.

Not only do you have to believe that Jesus Christ is both 100% God and 100% man, but you have to believe that He is a real, historical Person. Not that He is a legend or myth like Robin Hood or King Arthur. Not that He is a made-up Person to embody or personify eternal truths. Not that He appeared on earth as a Spirit with only the likeness but not the substance of human flesh. No, you have to accept intellectually that the God-man Jesus Christ really and truly lived and walked on the earth as accurately and truthfully recorded in Scripture.

But furthermore, you have to know that by His sufferings and death upon the Cross this God-man Jesus Christ fully and completely satisfied the wrath of God in your place. Not that Christ died as an example to us of how we should love God and others. Not that Christ died to make up what was lacking in your own merit or effort. Or, to put it another way, not that Christ paid 80% of your penalty and you still have to pay off the remaining 20%. But rather that Christ's vicarious sufferings and death fully and completely atoned for your sins.

Additionally, you have to intellectually accept that this God-man Jesus Christ not only drank your hell for you, but that on the third day He rose again from the dead. For the Apostle Paul tells us that, "if you confess with your mouth the Lord Jesu *and* believe in your heart that God has raised Him from the dead, you will be saved" (Rom. 10:9; emphasis added). Why is this important? Because, as Paul also tells us, "...if Christ is not risen, your faith is futile, you are still in your sins!" (1 Cor. 15:17). A dead Christ is a dead faith. If there is no resurrection, there is no salvation. Therefore, you must believe that Christ has destroyed the last enemy death (vs. 26); that "death is [now] swallowed up in victory" (vs. 54); and that through Christ we may also share in His victory over the grave (vs. 57).

And not that Christ was merely raised from the dead spiritually but not physically. Not simply that His ghost or spirit took on the appearance of human likeliness but without the substance of human flesh. But rather that Christ was bodily raised from the dead in the very same body with which He had lived, suffered, and died. A ghost masquerading as a living person saves no one, but only a resurrected, eternally-living body does. Only a pure, spotless sacrificial Lamb who fulfilled all righteousness— attested to as such by God the Father by bodily raising Him from the dead—saves anyone (Acts 2:22, 17:31). By being justified (i.e., declared righteous) by the Father (1 Tim. 3:16) by His resurrection, we are now justified by His righteousness (Rom. 4:25).

Finally, you have to intellectually accept that this God-man Jesus Christ is the exclusive means of salvation. For Peter declares that, "Nor is there salvation in any other, for there is no other name under heaven given among men by which we must be saved" (Acts 4:12). Jesus Himself maintained in John 14:6 that, "'I [alone] am the [only] way, the [only] truth, and the [only] life. [Absolutely] [n]o one comes to [God] the Father except through Me'" (Jn. 14:6). In several passages the Bible describes Jesus as the one, only, and final sacrifice for sins, of which no other can either be offered to or accepted by God (Heb. 7:27; see also Rom. 6:10; 1 Pet. 3:18).

In Romans 10 we read that apart from personal faith in God the Son there is no salvation:

> 13 For "everyone whosoever shall call upon the name of Yahweh shall be saved." 14 How then shall they call upon Him in whom they did not believe? And how shall they believe on Him of whom they did not hear? And how shall they hear apart from one heralding? 15 And how shall they herald, if they may not be sent? According as it has been written:
> "How beautiful the feet of those heralding the gospel of peace,
> of those heralding the good news of the good things!'
> (Rom. 10:13-15 NYLT)

In the second chapter of Philippians we read that:

> 9 Wherefore also God did highly exalt Him and gave to Him a name that is above every name, 10 that at the name of Jesus every knee may bow—of heavenlies, and earthlies, and those under the earth—11 and every tongue may confess that Jesus Messiah is Lord, to the glory of God the Father.
> (Phil. 2:9-11 NYLT)

Finally, in Psalm, chapter 2, we find God the Father promising victory to His Son over His enemies:

> [8] "Ask of Me, and I will give You
> The nations as Your inheritance,
> And for Your possession the ends of earth.
> [9] You rule them with a scepter of iron,
> As a vessel of a potter You crush them."
> [10] And now, O kings, act wisely,
> Be instructed, O judges of earth.
> [11] Serve Yahweh with fear,
> And rejoice with trembling.
> [12] Kiss the Son, lest He be angry,
> And you perish in the way,
> When His anger burns but a little,
> O the blessedness of all trusting in Him!
> (Ps. 2:8-12 NYLT)

Therefore, you must intellectually accept that you must either voluntarily bend the knee before Christ and acknowledge Him as your only Lord and God (Jn. 20:28) while you are still in the land of the living, or you will be forced to do so as your knee caps are broken before His eternal throne with His scepter of iron (Ps. 2:9; Rev. 2:27, 12:5, 19:15).

Concluding Implications:

In conclusion, there are, at a bare minimum, four facts that one must intellectually accept to have saving faith. First, that there is only one true and living God who is holy and righteous, just and good. Secondly, that not only is God true, but His Word is also true. Third, that one is a sinner who has fallen short of the glory of God and

91

therefore is under the just condemnation of an eternal hell. Fourth, that one may be saved from the wrath of God through Jesus Christ alone.

However, intellectual knowledge saves no one, for as Jacob tells us, "You—you believe that God is one. You do well, for so the demons believe—and they shudder!" (Jac. 2:19 NYLT). Not all faith is saving faith. Remember, Scripture describes us as spiritually dead—hardened and blinded in our deadness—with no capacity to see God as beautiful or to respond to the Gospel message. Consequently, as Jesus tells us, "unless one is born again, he cannot see the kingdom of God" (Jn. 3:3; see also vs. 5, 7). One does not savingly believe unless and until one has been born again. Next week's sermon, therefore will be on what happens when one is born again or regenerated; the saving faith that God gives us in that instant.

5 SOLA FIDE (PART 3)

I. *I*mpostor Faith. We ended the last chapter by noting that intellectual knowledge saves no one. Jesus' half-brother Jacob tells us that:

> "You—you believe that God is one. You do well, for so the demons believe—and they shudder!"
>
> (Jac. 2:19 NYLT)

Not all faith is saving faith. The Bible tells us, for instance, that the Legion of demons who possessed the man who lived among the tombs cried out, "What have we to do with You, Jesus Son of God? Have You come here to torment us before the time?'" (Matt. 8:29; see also Mk. 5:7). Mark tells us of another demon who cried out, "'Let us alone! What have we to do with You, Jesus of Nazareth? Did you come to destroy us? I know who You are—the Holy One of God!" (Mk. 1:24; see also Lk. 4:34). In Acts 19:15 yet another demon declares that he knew who Jesus is.

But the intellectual belief of these demons avail them not. Not all faith is saving faith. We see this in Matthew 7, which we looked at in the last chapter, where Jesus warns that not everyone who calls Him, "Lord," is, in fact, a Christian:

> 21 "Not every one who is saying to Me, "Lord, Lord,' shall come into the kingdom of the heavens; but he who is doing the will of My Father who is in the heavens. 22 Many will say to Me in that day, 'Lord, Lord, have we not in

You name prophesied? And in Your name cast out demons? And in Your name done many mighty things?' [23] And then I will confess to them that, 'I never knew you, depart from Me you who are working lawlessness.'"

(Matt. 7:21-23 NYLT)

These CINOS—*C*hristians *i*n *N*ame *O*nly—may have faith. It doubtless may be sincere and passionate faith. It may even be in the right Person of Jesus Christ. But it is not saving faith.

So what separates saving faith from non-saving faith? What makes saving faith different from New Year's resolutions, good works, legalism, or a Twelve-Step Program? Or, to put it another way, what distinguishes saving faith from mere morality? What marks the difference between a Christian in Name Only and a Christian in reality? Remember the fifth type of impostor we talked about last week—the one who sees something attractive about Christ but simply goes through the motions? They believe with all their heart that Christ died for sinners, but they have yet to believe from the heart that Christ died for them personally. They have the outward trappings of Christ, but they do not yet have Christ Himself. In fact, they are deeply in love with Christianity and may even be willing to be martyred for it. They remain, however, impostors. So what separates such an impostor faith from an authentic faith?

The difference is that impostors, Christians in Name Only, legalists, all these share one thing in common—they have not yet been born again. Scripture describes us as spiritually dead—hardened and blinded in our deadness—with no capacity to see God as beautiful or to respond to

94

the Gospel message. We must, therefore, be raised form spiritual deadness to spiritual life. We see this in Ephesians 2:

> [1] You also, being dead in trespasses and sins, [2] in which you once did walk according to the age of this world, according to the ruler of the authority of the air, of the spirit that is now working in the sons of disobedience, [3] among whom also we all did walk once in the desires of our flesh, doing the will of the flesh and of the thoughts, and were by nature children of wrath, just as the others.
> [4] But God, being rich in mercy, because of His great love with which He loved us, [5] even being dead in the trespasses, did make us to live together with the Messiah, (by grace you are saved), [6] and did raise us up together, and did seat us together in the heavenly places in Messiah Jesus, [7] that He might show, in the ages that are coming, the exceeding riches of His grace in kindness toward us in Messiah Jesus.
>
> (Eph. 2:1-7 NYLT)

A years worth of sermons could be preached from this passage alone, but look with me at the first three verses where we find the Apostle Paul describing for believers their earlier state of unregeneration before their conversion:

- **Verse 1:** Dead in trespasses and sins.
- **Verse 2:** Sons of disobedience.

95

Then notice how Paul says fallen mankind, by their very nature, behave:

- **Verse 2:** Walking according to the course of this world;
- **Verse 2:** Walking according to Satan (the prince of the power of the air);
- **Verse 3:** Fulfilling the sinful desires of their flesh.

Then notice how the Apostle Paul concludes his description of the unregenerate in verse 3: that they are, *by nature*, children of wrath. Paul doesn't tell us that we became children of wrath by our wrong behavior. By our individual sins. By our evil deeds outweighing our good deeds. No, the Apostle tells us that, *by nature*, we were children of wrath. Owing to our very depraved, sinful nature which we inherited from our first parent Adam, we became the rightful objects of divine wrath from the moment of conception.

But then look with me at glorious Good News of verses four and five:

> 4 But God, being rich in mercy, because of His great agape with which He agaped us, 5 even being dead in the trespasses, did make us to live together with the Messiah, (by grace you are saved),

> (Eph. 2:4-5 NYLT)

This is the difference between a genuine believer and an impostor believer—God has raised the genuine believer to everlasting spiritual life whereas the impostor believer remains spiritually dead in their trespasses and sins. The difference, therefore, between an authentic believer and a fake believer—or a Mormon, or a Muslim, or a follower of a Native religion—is not merely that they may believe different things. It is that the genuine Christian has been born again while the others remain spiritually dead— hardened and blinded in their spiritual deadness. This new birth isn't optional. As Christ stood outside Lazarus' tomb in John 11 and cried out, "Come forth!", so He must do so in your heart in order for you to be saved.

In John, chapter 3, we read:

1 And there was a man of the Pharisees, Nicodemus his name, a ruler of the Jews. 2 This one came unto Him by night and said to Him, "Rabbi, we have known that You are a teacher that have come from God; for no one is able to do these signs that You do if God is not be with him."

3 Jesus answered and said to him, "Amen! Amen!—I say to you, if any one may not be born again from above, he is not able to behold the kingdom of God."

4 Nicodemus says to Him, "How is a man able to be born, being old? Is he able to enter a second time into the womb of his mother and to be born?"

5 Jesus answered, "Amen! Amen!—I say to you, if any one may not be born of water and the Spirit, he is not able to enter into the kingdom of God. 6 That which has been born of the flesh is flesh, and that which has been born of the Spirit is spirit. 7 You may not marvel that I said to you, it behoves you to be born again from above. 8 The Spirit blows where He wills, and you hear His voice, but

you have not known where He comes and where He goes. Thus is everyone who has been born of the Spirit."

(Jn. 3:1-8 NYLT)

This is perhaps the most famous passage on new birth found in the Bible. And here Jesus says in verse 3 and then again in verses 5 and 7 that a person cannot be saved unless and until he is first born again. The Greek word translated here in verses 3 and 7 as *again* is anothen, which most often is translated not as *again* but as *from above*. So here Jesus is emphatically stating that a person must be born again from above by the Holy Spirit in order to be a genuine, authentic believer. This isn't optional. You must be birthed by the Holy Spirit if you are to have any part in Christ.

And the reason for the necessity of new birth is given by Christ in verse 6—"that which is born of the flesh is flesh, that which is born of the Spirit is spirit." A dead person cannot give birth to a live person. A pig cannot give birth to a human, nor a horse beget a whale. Likewise, a sinner cannot give birth to a saint.

Another word for new birth is, literally, regeneration. We see this in Titus 3:

3 For we were once also foolish, disobedient, led astray, serving manifold desires and pleasures, living in malice and envy, abominable in hating one another. 4 But when the kindness and philanthropic love of God our Savior toward men did appear, 5 not by works in righteousness that we did, but according to His mercy He did save us, through the bathing of regeneration and the renewing of the Holy

Spirit, 6 which He poured upon us richly through Jesus Messiah our Savior, 7 that having been declared righteous by His grace we may become heirs according to the hope of life age-enduring.

(Titus 3:3-7 NYLT)

Like the passage from Ephesians 2 which we read earlier, here Paul in verse 3 is describing sinners before their conversion. But then notice in verse 5 how the Apostle describes how believers become justified and heirs according to the hope of eternal life—"through the bathing of regeneration and renewing of the Holy Spirit." The word *regeneration* comes from the Greek word paliggenesia, which literally means *birth again.* Again, therefore, we see the necessity of being born again from above by the Holy Spirit in order to be saved.\

Finally, look with me at 1 Peter, chapter 1, where we read:

3 Blessed is the God and Father of our Lord Jesus Messiah, who, according to the abundance of His mercy did beget us again to a living hope, through the resurrection of Jesus Messiah out of the dead, 4 to an inheritance incorruptible and undefiled and unfading, reserved in the heavens for you 5 who, in the power of God, are being guarded through faith unto salvation ready to be revealed in the last time...

23 being begotten again, not out of corruptible seed but incorruptible, through the word of God which is living and remaining to the age.

(1 Pet 1:3-5, 23 NYLT)

Verse 3 tells us that God has begotten believers again to a living hope, and verse 23 declares that they have been begotten through the word of God. The phrase *beget again* of verse 3 and *begotten again* of verse 23 is the same Greek word—anagennao, which means to give birth again or from above. Again, therefore, we see the necessity of being born again from above by the Holy Spirit in order to be saved.

II. Born Again Produces Repentance & Faith. So what happens when you are born again from above by the Holy Spirit? 2 Corinthians, chapter 4, provides us with the most exhaustive definition found in Scripture:

> 3 But if also our gospel is veiled, it is veiled in those perishing— 4 in whom the god of this age did blind the minds of the unbelieving— that there does not shine forth to them the enlightening of the gospel of the glory of the Messiah, who is the image of God. 5 For we do not herald ourselves, but Messiah Jesus as Lord, and ourselves as your slaves because of Jesus. 6 Because it is God who said, "Out of darkness light is to shine," who did shine in our hearts for the enlightening of the knowledge of the glory of God in the face of Jesus Messiah.
>
> (2 Cor. 4:3-6 NYLT)

We are by nature spiritually dead—blinded and hardened in our deadness—with no capacity to understand or receive the things of God. As the Apostle Paul tells us, "...the natural man does not receive the things of the Spirit of God, for they are foolishness to him, nor can he know them, because they are spiritually discerned" (1 Cor. 2:14). But as we just read in verse 6 of 2 Corinthians, chapter 4, that just as "God who said, 'Out of darkness light is to shine' at the creation of the universe, so at the moment of new birth He "did shine in our hearts for the enlightening of the knowledge of the glory of God in the face of Jesus Messiah."

At new birth, therefore, the spiritually blind now see! The spiritually dead now live! As the prolific hymn writer Charles Wesley put it in the fourth stanza of his famous hymn *And Can It Be?*:

> 4 Long my imprisoned spirit lay
> Fast bound in sin and nature's night;
> Thine eye diffused a quick'ning ray,
> I woke, the dungeon flamed with light;
> My chains fell off, my heart was free;
> I rose, went forth and followed Thee.

To use a contemporary analogy from the 1999 blockbuster movie *The Matrix*, all mankind by nature live in a spiritual matrix—completely oblivious to eternal truths. We are blinded to the spiritual realities around us. Like the computers in the movie, the god of this world—the devil—has blinded our hearts to the Real (2 Cor. 4:4). But just as Neil took the blue pill and was awakened out of his stupor to see the world as it really was, so new birth awakens an individual to the spiritual world as it really is.

In Isaiah, chapter 42, we find God describing the mission of His coming Messiah—our Lord Jesus Christ:

> 5 Thus said Yahweh God Jehovah,

Preparing the heavens and stretching them out,
Spreading out the earth and its productions,
Giving breath to the people on it,
And spirit to those walking in it.
6 "I, Yahweh, did call You in righteousness,
And I lay hold on Your hand,
And keep You and I give You for a covenant of a people,
And a light of nations,
7 To open the eyes of the blind,
To bring forth from prison the bound one,
From the house of restraint those sitting in darkness.
8 I am Yahweh, this is My name,
And My glory to another I give not,
Nor My praise to graven images.
9 Behold!—the former things have come,
And new things I am declaring,
Before they spring up I cause you to hear."

(Is. 42:5-9 NYLT)

The power of the Gospel of Christ is to be a light to open blind eyes and to bring out prisoners who once sat in the darkness of their prison. In Acts, chapter 26, we find the Apostle Paul describing his conversion and commissioning as a minister of the Gospel:

12 "In which things, also, going on to Damascus with authority and commission from the chief priests, 13 at midday, I saw in the way, O king, out of heaven a light—above the brightness of the sun— shining round about me and those going on with me. 14 And we all

having fallen to the earth, I heard a voice speaking unto me, and saying in the Hebrew tongue, 'Saul, Saul, why do you persecute Me? It is hard for you to kick against stings!' [15] And I said, 'Who are you, Lord?' And He said, 'I am Jesus whom you persecute.[16] But rise and stand upon your feet, for this I appeared to you—to appoint you an officer and a witness both of the things you see and of the things which I will appear to you, [17] delivering you from the people and the ethnic groups to whom now I send you, [18] to open their eyes, to turn them from darkness to light, and from the authority of the Adversary unto God, for their receiving forgiveness of sins and a lot among those having been sanctified by faith that is toward Me.'"

(Acts 26:12-18 NYLT)

Once again we see that the power of the Gospel of Christ is to open eyes and turn people from darkness to light, from the power of Satan to God, that they might be forgiven and become heirs of God. Conversion, therefore, is when a person sees God as holy and righteous and worthy of all worship, himself as sinful and vile and worthy of all hell, but Christ's blood and righteousness as his precious and beautiful atonement. Our eyes our opened to see divine glories as the love of God is poured out into our hearts (Rom. 5:5). By the Holy Spirit's quickening at the moment of regeneration, Christ suddenly becomes irresistibly beautiful to us as we simultaneously "repent and believe the Gospel" (Mk. 1:15) and are justified—or declared righteous with Christ's righteousness—by God.

Repentance and faith are two sides of the same coin called conversion. You cannot have one without the other; they are inseparable. If you have faith without repentance, you do not have saving faith. You merely have head knowledge without godly sorrow for your sinfulness. And if you have repentance without faith, you do not have saving faith. Rather, you have remorse without hope; penitence without assurance. In fact, these two terms—repentance and faith—are used interchangeably in the New Testament for saving faith.

For instance, we read in Matthew, chapter 3:

> [1] And in those days come John the Baptist, heralding in the wilderness of Judea [2] and saying, "Repent, for the kingdom of the heavens has come near!"
>
> (Matt. 3:1-2 NYLT)

Dropping down to verse 8, John tells the crowds to, "bear fruits worthy of repentance!" In the next chapter, we read: "From that time Jesus began to preach and to say, 'Repent, for the kingdom of heaven is at hand!'" (Matt. 4:17). A few chapters later we find:

> [12] And Jesus having heard, said to them, "They who are whole have no need of a physician, but they who are ill. [13] But having gone, learn you what this means: 'Mercy I desire, and not sacrifice.' For I did not come to call righteous men, but sinners, to repentance."
>
> (Matt. 9:12-13 NYLT; see also Lk. 5:31)

In Mark, chapter 6, Jesus commissioned His Twelve Apostles to proclaim the Gospel, and verse 12 tells us that, "...they went out and preached that people should repent." In Luke, chapter 13, we read:

> [1] And there were present at that time certain men, telling Him about the Galileans whose blood Pilate did mingle with their sacrifices. [2] And Jesus answering said to them, "Think you that these Galileans became sinners beyond all the Galileans, because they have suffered such things? [3] No. I say to you, but if you may not repent, even so all of you shall perish. [4] Or those eighteen on whom the tower in Siloam fell and killed them, do you think that these became debtors beyond all men who are dwelling in Jerusalem? [5] No. I say to you, but if you may not repent, all of you in like manner shall perish."
>
> (Lk. 13:1-5 NYLT)

Then a few chapters over in Luke we find Christ giving two parables:

> [4] "What man of you, having a hundred sheep, and having lost one out of them, does not leave behind the ninety-nine in the wilderness, and go on after the lost one until he may find it? [5] And having found it, he lays it on his shoulders, rejoicing. [6] And having come to the house, he calls together his friends and neighbors, saying to them, 'Rejoice with me, because I found my sheep—the lost one!' [7] I say to you that in the same way there shall be

joy in the heaven over one sinner repenting, rather than over ninety-nine righteous men who have no need of reformation.

8 Or what woman having ten drachmas, if she may lose one drachma, doth not light a lamp, sweep the house, and seek carefully until she may find? 9 And having found is, she calls together her friends and neighbors, saying, 'Rejoice with me, for I found the drachma that I lost.' 10 So I say to you, joy comes before the angelic messengers of God over one sinner repenting."

(Lk. 15:4-10 NYLT)

Finally, in Luke, chapter 24, we read of Christ giving His disciples the Great Commission:

46 And He said to them, "Thus it has been written, and thus it was behoving the Messiah to suffer, and to rise out of the dead the third day, 47 and repentance and remission of sins to be heralded in His name to all ethnic groups, beginning at Jerusalem. 48 And you are witnesses of these things. 49 And, behold! —I send the Promise of My Father upon you, but you—abide in the city of Jerusalem until you should be clothed with power from on high."

(Lk. 24:46-49 NYLT)

There are many other passages—such as Acts 2:38, 3:19, 11:18, and 17:30—that could be cited as well. But because space is limited, I simply want to draw your attention to four more that clearly and explicitly show how repentance and faith are used interchangeably for saving faith. In Mark 1 we find Jesus beginning His earthly ministry by crying out, "The time if fulfilled, and the kingdom of God is at hand. Repent, and believe the Gospel!" (Mk. 1:15).

Then in Acts, chapter 20, while in the midst of his farewell address to the Ephesian elders we find Paul saying, that he, "testif[ied] to Jews, and also to Greeks, repentance toward God and faith toward our Lord Jesus Christ" (Acts 20:21). A few chapters later in Acts 26, we read:

> [19] "Whereupon, King Agrippa, I was not disobedient to the heavenly vision, [20] but heralded—first to those in Damascus, and then to those in Jerusalem and to all the region of Judea, and then to the ethnic groups —that they should repent and to turn back to God, doing works worthy of repentance."
>
> (Acts 26:19-20 NYLT)

"Repent, turn to God, and do works befitting [or demonstrating] repentance" (vs. 20). That is conversion. And we see it once more in Paul's description of the conversion of the Thessalonian believers as "turn[ing] to God from idols to serve the living and true God" (1 Thess. 1:9).

These two terms—repentance and faith—are synonymous for new birth:

- **Mark 1:15:** "Repent and believe the Gospel!"
- **Acts 20:21:** "Repentance towards God and faith toward our Lord Jesus Christ."

- **Acts 26:19:** "Repent and to turn back to God, doing works worthy of repentance."
- **1 Thess. 1:9:** "Turn to God from idols."

Saving faith, therefore, is a turning to Christ in belief as one forsakes and repents of their sins. You cannot have one without the other, or you do not have saving faith. Genuine faith, authentic faith, saving faith is a penitent faith.

III. Repentance. What, then is repentance? In the last chapter we saw that there was an impostor faith in which a professing Christian embraces Christ as their ticket out of hell, but nothing more. They come under just enough conviction of sin to know they are not at peace with God and, consequently, in danger of hell fire upon drawing their last breath. But the problem with their repentance is that they don't actually hate their sins, they just simply don't want to go to hell. And if it were possible, they would still want their sins if they could still escape hell. Sadly, their conviction of sin is merely that of worldly sorrow—that of a criminal sorry that he got caught but who would do it again in a heartbeat if he thought he could get away with it.

Birthed out of Love. Godly sorrow, in contrast, is rooted and grounded in love for God. It is when the Holy Spirit opens the eyes of the heart through new birth and an individual sees God as holy and righteous, just and good, loving and wrathful. He sees God as worthy of all of his love, worship, and obedience. He sees God as the most supremely valuable treasure in the entire universe, and cries out like the angels before the throne of God in Isaiah 6, "Holy, Holy, Holy is Yahweh Sabaoth!" (Is. 6:3 NYLT).

And at the same time he sees himself as a wretched and vile sinner without any defense or justification before such a holy God. Like Isaiah the prophet who in a vision saw God seated in Hs throne room (Is. 6:5), a penitent man cries out, "Woe is me, for I am a man with an unclean heart!" And like the crowds at Pentecost who were stabbed through the heart with godly sorrow, he cries out, "What must I do to be saved?" (Acts 2:37). And like the Old Testament saints in Joel, he rends his heart and turns to God with all of his heart (Joel 2:12-13).

At the moment of new birth, the Holy Spirit begets or creates in him a new nature. As the Apostle Paul exclaims, "So that if anyone is in Messiah, he is a new creature; the old things did pass away, behold!—all things have become new!" (2 Cor. 5:17). He now loves the God he once hated, and hates the sin he once loved. He has experienced nothing less than a heart transplant. In Ezekiel, chapter 11, we find Yahweh speaking:

> [19] And I have given to them one heart, and a new spirit I do give in your midst, and I have turned the heart of stone out of their flesh, and I have given to them a heart of flesh, [20] so that in My statutes they walk, and My judgments they keep, and have done them; and they have been to Me for a people, and I am to them for God.
>
> (Ezek. 11:19-20 NYLT)

A few chapters later, in Ezekiel 36, we read:

> [25] And I have sprinkled over you clean water, and you have been clean; I cleanse you from all your uncleannesses and from all your idols. [26] And I have given to you a new heart, and a new spirit I give in your midst, and I have

turned aside the heart of stone out of your
flesh, and I have given to you a heart of flesh.
27 And My Spirit I give in your midst, and I
have done this so that in My statutes you walk,
and My judgments you keep, and have done
them...
31 And you have remembered your ways that
are evil, and your doings that are not good,
and have been loathsome in your own faces—
for your iniquities and for your abominations.

(Ezek. 36:25-27, 31 NYLT)

At the moment of new birth God gives us His Spirit
and His heart (Ezek. 11:19, 36:26), which has two effects.
The first is that it produces repentance. We see this in
verse 31—"[a]nd you have remembered your ways that are
evil, and your doings that are not good, and have been
loathsome in your own faces—for your iniquities and for
your abominations" (Ezek. 33:31 NYLT). But the second
effect is the spiritual life, the spiritual desire, the spiritual
power to walk in holiness. We see this in verse 27: "And
My Spirit I give in your midst, and *I have done this* so that
in My statutes *you walk*, and My judgments *you keep*, and
have done them" (emphasis added; see also 11:20).

I often illustrate man's sin nature with a pig analogy:
let's pretend that on my right hand I had a gourmet meal
freshly prepared and laid out on the finest of china, and on
my left hand I had pig slop. If I brought a hog into this
room, which meal do you think he is going to go to? It is a
hog. It doesn't care about the culinary arts or fine dining, it
wants slop. He was conceived and born with a desire for
filth. And so were we.

But, to build on the analogy, what would happen if by
snapping my fingers I was able to instantaneously turn the

pig into a man? He would look at himself and the filth he was feasting upon in horror and disgust. Nay, in repulsion. He would be sick to his stomach at what he had just eaten. He would be embarrassed and ashamed at what he had done. He would loath himself and hate his old pig nature.

Or, to use another analogy, let's imagine that you lived in a pitch black cave. Your pets were rats, who in your blindness you thought were as adorable as dogs. Your idea of a beautiful bird were the grotesque bats flying around your head. Your idea of a good time is making mud pies in the ground. And your idea of beautiful jewelry is an ebony broach that you wear around your neck. Until suddenly one day the walls of the cave collapse, and as the sunlight floods in you realize that all the things you loved and cherished were hideous. You killed all the bats and rats you could find. You saw that the sandy beaches of the seashore nearby were perfect for building sandcastles. In horror you realized that the ebony broach you so prized was in fact a cockroach.

That is exactly what happens at new birth. The believer's new nature, his new heart, immediately begins to love the things that God loves and hate the things that God hates. And, as a result, he is ashamed, disgusted, and revolted at his old sin nature. He experiences godly sorrow over his sin because it blasphemes, denigrates, and grieves God's worth. He repents of his sin because it is an affront to God's holiness. His hates his sin because God hates it.

He loathes his sin because it held Christ upon the cross of Calvary. Because he was among those who cried out to Pontius Pilate, "Crucify Him! Crucify Him!" Because he was among those who scourged Christ ruthlessly with a Cat of Nine Tails. Because he was among those who mockingly shoved a crown of thorns upon Christ's head, beat Him, and ridiculed Him. Because he was among those who drove the nails into Christ's wrists and feet. Because he were among those who blasphemed Christ and denied His deity.

Forsaking Self-Idolatry. But as important, vital, and necessary as this change of heart producing love for God which results in hatred of sin is, saving, penitent faith is more than that. Or, rather, it is more specific than that. Saving, penitent faith specifically occurs when one forsakes salvation by self-idolatry. It is when one gives up trying to earn their way to heaven and trusts Christ and Christ alone as their all-sufficient righteousness.

Saving, penitent faith repents of any self-righteousness on your part. It renounces any notion that you are or could ever become good enough for God. It admits that you are completely powerless to earn your own salvation. It confesses that just as "the Ethiopian [cannot] change his skin or the leopard its spots[, n]either can you do good who are accustomed to doing evil" (Prov. 13:23). It acknowledges that, "The heart is deceitful above all things, and desperately wicked" (Jer. 17:9). It echos with the author of Job when he writes, "What is man that he could become pure?" (Job 15:14; see also Job 25:4), for "who can make something pure out of what is impure? No one" (Job 14:4). It confesses to God that one cannot say, I have made my heart pure; I am clean and without sin (Prov. 20:8). Like Isaiah the prophet, it admits that, "All of us have become like one who is unclean, and all our righteous acts are like menstrual rags" (Is. 64:6 NYLT).

In Galatians, the Apostle Paul writes:

> **2** [16] Having known also that a man is not declared righteous by works of the law but through faith in Jesus Messiah, even we who

in Messiah Jesus did believe, that we might be declared righteous by the faith in Messiah and not by works of the law, for by works of the law no flesh shall be declared righteous....

[21] I do not set aside the grace of God, for if righteousness be through the law, then Messiah died in vain...

3 [11] And that by the law no one is declared righteous with God is evident, because "The righteous shall live by faith."

(Gal. 2:16, 21, 3:11 NYLT; see also Rom. 3:30, 28)

This is what saving repentance confesses. Saving, penitent faith, therefore, is a despairing hopelessness, a desperate helplessness. It is coming to a complete end of oneself; a total and final giving up on one's ability to save oneself. It is repenting of any and all attempts at legalism, good works, New Year's resolutions, and tears in an effort to earn, in whole or in part, one's salvation. Like the hymn *Rock of Ages*, a born again man confesses:

[2] Not the labor of my hands
Can fulfill Thy law's demands;
Could my zeal no respite know,
Could my tears forever flow,
All could never sin erase,
Thou must save, and save by grace.
[3] Nothing in my hands I bring,
Simply to Thy cross I cling;

A man regenerated by the Holy Spirit cries out in repentance, "God forbid that I should boast except in the cross of our Lord Jesus Christ!" (Gal. 6:14). A person is not born again, is not regenerate, is not converted, is not a Christian, unless and until they have repented of any and all self-righteousness. Of self-goodness. Of earning their way to heaven. Of believing that God owes them anything but eternal damnation. If you have not yet reached this point of utter despair and hopelessness, of utter lack of trust and faith, in yourself, you are not saved. Period.

IV. Faith. But then the flip side of saving repentance—the other side of the coin called conversion—is saving faith. It is simultaneously taking one's trust, one's confidence, one's hope off of one's own righteousness and instead placing it in that of Christ and Christ alone. There is no time lapse between saving repentance and saving faith. They are the same act of penitent faith in which you cannot have one without the other.

Saving faith is a desperate faith. It is born out of the despairing hopelessness, the desperate helplessness, of saving repentance. It is an earnest coming to God in simple, childlike faith, trusting that it is only through the obedient life and the shed blood of this God-man Jesus Christ that he has forgiveness of sins (John 1:12, 3:17-18, 5:24, 6:40, 47, 11:25-26; Acts 16:31; Romans 10:13; Hebrews 9:26, 28). It is a coming to God in brokenness and poverty of spirit, mourning the sin of his heart (Ps. 34:18, 38:18; Isaiah 57:13, 66:1-2; Matt. 5:3-4; 2 Cor. 7:10) and trusting that one is clothed with Christ's righteousness and holiness alone (2 Cor. 5:21. It is solely looking unto Jesus as the initiator and consummator of his faith (Heb. 12:2).

And this is not a faith of wishful thinking. It is not a guestimation. It is not a passing wish that one will make it to heaven. No! Saving, penitent faith is always accompanied by a measure of felt, knowable assurance that, in fact, his sins are forgiven, that he is reconciled and at peace with God, and that this will result in his ultimate salvation. This is not a mere intellectual consent that sins may be forgiven or even that his sins are forgiven, but rather it is a personal, intimate, experimental, tangible appropriation of forgiveness and life in Christ. In saving faith, there is no longer any fear, guilt, or shame of death, hell, judgment, and condemnation.

We see this clearly in the eleventh chapter of Hebrews:

> [1] Now faith is the title-deed of things hoped for, the proof of matters not seen. [2] For by this the elders obtained a good testimony. [3] By faith we understand the ages to have been prepared by a saying of God, in regard to the things seen not having come out of things appearing...[6] But apart from faith it is impossible to please well, for it behoves him who is coming to God to believe that He is, and to those earnestly seeking Him He becomes a paymaster.
>
> (Heb. 11:1-3, 6 NYLT)

What is faith? The Greek word translated here *title-deed* is hypostasis, which literally means to *stand under a title dead*. Or, to put it another way, it is the appropriating or substantiating—or a claiming a right to—a guaranteed agreement or promise. So, to put it into practical terms, faith is presenting a check at the bank with full confidence that it will be deposited into your account. That is what faith is—the appropriating or claiming the promises of God in full confidence of their fulfillment. In fact, the Greek word translated here in verse 1 as *hoped for* is elpizo, which means *expected* or *anticipated*. Faith is claiming the promises of God in full expectation that they will be fulfilled. It is a substantiation, a foretaste, a realization of future fulfillment.

And look at the rest of verse 1: "faith is...the proof of things not seen." The Greek word translated here as *proof* is elegchos, which means *evidence* or *conviction*. Faith is the God-given internal persuasion of the unseen realities of God's promises. Of the truthworthiness of God's Word. It is being born again by the Holy Spirit with new eyes to grasp divine glories. To see the unseen. To live in the invisible. And to know beyond all doubt that it is far more real than anything we can see with our physical eyes.

Therefore, saving faith is always accompanied by a measure—though it be as small as a fraction of a mustard seed—of assurance. Faith is the conviction, being sure, reality of, substance, guarantee, foretaste, and resolute confidence of the personal application of the thing promised, without which faith does not exist but is rather merely a hopeless intellectual assent shared by demons. Faith is an experience that lives, moves, and has its being in the unseen realities of Scriptural promises.

Furthermore, regeneration is the creation of a new man, a passing from death to life, the shinning forth of the light of the knowledge of the glory of God in the face of Jesus Christ in one's heart; it is no more conceivable, therefore, to experience an earthquake, tornado, tsunami, or hurricane and not realize it than it is to be born again by the power of the living God and not know it. If one does not personally and experimentally know that Jesus Christ is in them, they are reprobate—still dead in their trespasses and sins and remain under God's wrath. A born again man may have the assurance of his salvation shaken and diminished at different times and in different ways, but yet he will never be without at least a seed of unbreakable, imperishable assurance of salvation.

Concluding Implications:

In conclusion, at new birth—the moment of regeneration or conversion—an individual is created anew by the Holy Spirit into a new creation in which two things happen. The first is that, out of love for God, he now hates his sin and repents and despairs of his self-idolatrous attempts to earn his salvation. And, secondly and simultaneously, he now, with full confidence, places his sole hope of salvation in Christ and Christ alone. And such receiving of Christ's love vanquishes all fear of death and hell. New birth creates saving, penitent faith, by which alone a man is justified, or declared righteous, by God. Without this new birth, there is no hope for salvation.

In Genesis, chapter 2, we read of God's creation of man:

> And Yahweh God forms the man—dust from the ground, and breaths into his nostrils the breath of life, and the man becomes a living creature.
>
> (Gen. 2:7 NYLT)

When God formed Adam, he was nothing more than a clump of earth. He may have looked like a man. But he had no life in him. His heart did not beat. His lungs did not breath. His brain did not think. But when Yahweh breathed into his nostrils the breath of life, the man became a living being (vs. 7; see also Ezek. 37:9-10).

And then in John, chapter 20, we read:

²¹ Jesus, therefore, said to them again, "Peace to you! According as the Father has sent Me, I also send you." ²² And having said this, He breathed on them, and says to them, "Receive the Holy Spirit."

(Jn. 20:21-22 NYLT)

That is conversion. Unbelievers may look alive, but they are merely the walking dead; living corpses. But then God breathes the Holy Spirit into the heart of a spiritually dead person—blinded and hardened in their deadness—and makes them alive in Christ; new creations with the power and desire to exercise saving, penitent faith. Without this new birth, you are still dead in your trespasses and sins on your way to hell for all eternity. Therefore, if you have not yet been born again, I plead with you to "repent and believe the Gospel" today (Mk. 1:15)!

6 SOLA FIDE (PART 4)

We have been spending the last several chapters on the doctrine of *Sola Fide*—that justification is by grace alone through faith alone. We have seen that this free gift—in which our sin is imputed to Christ and He experienced hell for it and His righteousness is imputed to us and we live eternally through it—is appropriated by the instrument or agency of faith. And it is by faith alone to the exclusion of works, for the two are mutually incompatible. It is either 100% faith or 100% works. And this faith by which we are saved is not something that we mustered up on our own but, rather, is solely a gracious gift from God so that no man may boast in His presence.

And we examined the question of what is saving faith by first examining five different types of impostor faith: (1) one who thinks of Christ as his pimp daddy or enabler who will give them their best life now; (2) one who simply embraces Christ as their ticket to heaven, but nothing more; (3) one who embraces Christ as their ticket out of hell, but nothing more; (4) one who embraces Christ, but not Christ alone; and, finally, (5) one who sees something attractive about Christ but simply goes through the motions.

We also saw that, at a bare minimum, there are four facts that one must intellectually accept to have saving faith. First, that there is only one true and living God who is holy and righteous, just and good. Secondly, that not only is God true, but His Word is also true. Third, that one is a sinner who has fallen short of the glory of God and therefore is under the just condemnation of an eternal hell. Fourth, that one may be saved from the wrath of God through Jesus Christ alone.

Then we saw that intellectual knowledge saves no one. Not all faith is saving faith. The difference between Christians in Name Only (CINOs) and Christians in reality is that the former have not yet been born again. Remember that Scripture describes us as spiritually dead —hardened and blinded in our deadness—with no capacity to see God as beautiful or to respond to the Gospel message. We must, therefore, be raised form spiritual deadness. We must be born again from above by the Holy Spirit in order to have the ability, power, and desire to exercise saving, penitent faith.

Conversion—or new birth or regeneration—is when a person sees God as holy and righteous and worthy of all worship, himself as sinful and vile and worthy of all hell, but Christ's blood and righteousness as his precious and beautiful atonement. Our eyes our opened to see divine glories as the love of God is poured out into our hearts (Rom. 5:5). By the Holy Spirit's quickening at the moment of regeneration, Christ suddenly becomes irresistibly beautiful to us as we simultaneously "repent and believe the Gospel" (Mk. 1:15) and are justified—or declared righteous with Christ's righteousness—by God.

Furthermore, we saw that saving, penitent faith specifically occurs when one forsakes salvation by self-idolatry. It is when one gives up trying to earn their way to heaven and trusts Christ and Christ alone as their all-sufficient righteousness. Saving, penitent faith, therefore, is a despairing hopelessness, a desperate helplessness. It is coming to a complete end of oneself; a total and final giving up on one's ability to save oneself. But then the flip side of saving repentance—the other side of the coin called conversion—is saving faith. It is simultaneously taking one's trust, one's confidence, one's hope off of one's own righteousness and instead placing it in that of

Christ and Christ alone. There is no time lapse between saving repentance and saving faith. They are the same act of penitent faith in which you cannot have one without the other.

I. The Necessity of Treasuring Christ. But is that it? Is that all saving faith is? Is it merely coming to Christ as Savior but nothing more? Is our concern at conversion simply about escaping hell and gaining heaven but nothing more? Remember the two types of impostor Christians we discussed?

The first is one who simply embraces Christ as their ticket to heaven, but nothing more. They don't echo with the Apostle that, "for me to live is Christ, and to die is gain" (Phil. 1:21) out of a desire to be with Christ forever. Rather, they simply want a carefree eternity; a ceaseless paradise. An endless party with family and friends in which they get to live out their most selfish imaginations for all eternity. They don't want heaven because Christ is there and, if they were honest, they would prefer He not be there because He would not approve of their definition of fun. They don't want to feast their souls on the infinite Christ, but rather indulge their sinful lusts upon infinite self-idolatry.

And the other type of impostor is the one who embraces Christ as their ticket out of hell, but nothing more. They have come under just enough conviction of sin to know they are not at peace with God and, consequently, in danger of hell fire upon drawing their last breath. But they in fact do not hate their sins, but merely don't want to go to hell. And if possible, they would still want their sins if they could still escape hell.

But if saving faith is all about escaping hell and gaining heaven, how is it different from these two types of impostor faith? If you come to Christ as Savior but as nothing more, how is that not an impostor faith? If you come to Christ merely as Savior but nothing more, you do not love Christ. You do not treasure Him. You have no real affection for Him. Rather, if you come to Christ merely as Savior but nothing more, you in fact are treasuring escaping hell and a pain-free eternity in heaven far more than you are treasuring Christ.

To illustrate, imagine that you were convicted by a jury of first-degree murder and were facing the death sentence. But when you showed up at the sentencing hearing, the judge suddenly declares you not guilty and orders your immediate release from custody. If you have any affection towards the judge, it merely one of gratitude. You may send him an annual Christmas card. You might even buy him a birthday present every year. But with each year that passes he means less and less to you. He was just a get out of jail free card to you and nothing more. Your affection towards him, if you had any at all, is not love-producing obedience.

Or, imagine that you married primarily for money, or prestige, or power, or duty. Your view of your spouse is simply that as a means, a tool, as someone useful to obtain something that you treasure as far more superior instead. They are not the prize of your heart; rather, they are the ticket to win the prize of your heart. And when they have served their purpose, they may be tossed away and discarded as easily as you do a used kleenex.

Similarly, faith that merely embraces Christ as Savior but as nothing more is an impostor faith. Why? For the fundamental reason that it treats Christ simply as a means, as a tool, as Someone useful to obtain something that the person treasures more than Christ—namely, escape from hell and a pain-free eternity. But as St. Augustine put it,

"He loves Thee too little who loves anything together with Thee, which he loves not for Thy sake." Or to put it in modern vernacular, loving Christ for His salvation without loving Him for His infinite worth is not truly loving Christ. Treasuring Christ, therefore, solely to escape hell is not saving faith. Treasuring Christ solely to gain a pain-free heaven is not saving faith.

II. The Scripture Definition of Saving Faith— Treasuring Christ. Rather, Scripture defines saving faith as that which receives as one's supreme treasure all that God is in Christ for them in order to make much of God. That's a lot to digest so we will take it apart phrase by phrase.

II.A. Receives. First, saving faith is a receiving of Christ. We read in John, chapter 1, that:

> 10 He was in the world, and the world was made through Him, and the world *did not know Him*. 11 To His own He came, and His own *did not receive Him*. 12 But as many *as did receive Him*, to them He gave authority to become sons of God, to those *believing in His name*: 13 who were begotten, not of bloods, nor of the will of flesh, nor of the will of man, but of God.
>
> (Jn. 1:10-13 NYLT; emphasis added)

Look at the terms used by John for faith in this one passage alone. He describes unbelief in verse 10 as not knowing Christ, and in verse 11 as not receiving Him. Then, in contrast, in verse 12 he describes faith as both receiving Christ and believing in Him. So to summarize from this passage, saving faith is:

- **Verse 10:** Knowing Christ (see also Jn. 17:3).
- **Verse 11 & 12:** Receiving Christ.
- **Verse 12:** Believing Christ.

What I want to highlight for the moment, however, is John's use of the word *receive* for saving faith. Saving faith is a reception, an accepting, a receiving. It is not a work. Rather, it ceases from all working—all earning, all striving—to save oneself and instead accepts Christ's completed work on one's behalf. Saving faith is the instrument by which we are united with Christ so that His righteousness is imputed to us and we live eternally through it. Saving faith, therefore, is not a giving but a receiving; not an acting but an accepting of another's performance; not fruit itself but the union with the Good Tree, the Good Vine, of Jesus Christ.

II.B. Supreme Treasure. Secondly, then, how does saving faith receive Christ? As one's supreme treasure. As one's supreme love. As one's supreme delight. As one's supreme satisfaction and rest.

II.B.1. Supreme Treasure. In Matthew, chapter 13, we read:

> [44] "Again, the kingdom of the heavens is like treasure hidden in the field, which a man having found hide, and from his joy goes and sells all—as much as he has—and buys that field.

45 "Again, the kingdom of the heavens is like to a man, a merchant, seeking good pearls, 46 who, having found one pearl of great price, having gone away, has sold all—as much as he had—and bought it.

(Matt. 13:44-46 NYLT)

Saving faith, therefore, seizes upon Christ as supremely valuable. At the moment of conversion, a born-again man sees Christ as a hidden treasure, a pearl of unfathomable worth, (2 Cor. 4:4, 6) for whom he joyfully renounces all his worldly treasures to obtain. We see this in the testimony of the Apostle Paul in Philippians 3:

7 But what things were to me gains, these I have counted, because of Messiah, loss. 8 Yes, indeed, and I count all things to be loss, because of the excellency of the knowledge of Messiah Jesus my Lord, because of whom I suffered the loss of all things, and do count them to be dung, that I may gain Messiah, 9 and be found in Him, not having my own righteousness, which is of the law, but that which is through faith in Christ—the righteousness that is from God by faith.

(Phil. 3:7-9 NYLT)

At the moment of conversion, a born-again man sees everything he once held dear as rubbish compared to Christ. His treasure, like Paul's, is now to gain Christ and be found in Him. As Peter put it, "Therefore, to you who believe He is precious" (1 Pet. 2:7). Saving faith, therefore, treasures Christ, prizes Christ, values Christ supremely. It occurs when He becomes more precious to you than anything that life has to offer or that death can take away. He becomes your magnificent obsession. He becomes, as God promised Abraham, your "exceedingly great reward" (Gen. 15:1).

II.B.2. Supreme Love. Saving faith is also receiving Christ as one's supreme love. Look with me at 1 Corinthians 16:

> If anyone does not brotherly love the Lord Jesus Messiah, let him be anathema! Maranatha—O Lord come!
>
> (1 Cor. 16:22 NYLT)

The Apostle Paul cannot be more clearer that the main element of saving faith is love than he is here: if you do not love Christ, you have never had saving faith and are damned. In John, chapter 5, we read:

> [41] "I do not receive glory from man. [42] But I have known you, that the agape of God you have not in yourselves. [43] I have come in the name of My Father, and you do not receive Me; if another may come in his own name, him you will receive. [44] How are you able to believe, who are receiving glory from one another, and you do not seek the glory that is from the only God?"
>
> (Jn. 5:41-44 NYLT)

Notice, first, that in verse 43 Christ describes saving faith as receiving Him. This is what we saw earlier in John 1:10-13 where receiving Christ is synonymous with believing in Him. But then notice in this passage the other terms Christ uses for saving faith—believing and love of God. Receiving, believing in, and love for Christ are all used here by Christ to describe saving faith.

Then let's look a few pages over in John 3:

> [18] "He who is believing in Him is not judged, but he who is not believing has been judged already, because he has not believed in the name of the only begotten Son of God. [19] And this is the judgment, that the light has come to the world, and men did love the darkness rather than the light, for their works were evil."
>
> (Jn. 3:18-19 NYLT)

Here Christ contrasts those who believe in Him with those who love darkness rather than light. Or, to put it another way, to believe in Christ is to love the light. And, as Christ told us in John 8:12, He is the light of the world. So to believe in Christ is to love Christ, and to not believe in Christ is not to love Christ. Saving faith, therefore, is love for Christ.

Similarly, in 2 Thessalonians, chapter 2, the Apostle Paul describes what will happen to non-believers:

> [9] whose presence is according to the working of the Adversary, in all power, and signs, and lying wonders, [10] and in all unrighteous deceitfulness in those perishing, because they did not receive the love of the truth for their being saved.
>
> (2 Thess. 2:9-10 NYLT)

Here again we see that those who do not believe described as those who do not receive the love of the truth.

So to believe in Christ is to love the truth. And as Jesus told us in John 14:6, He alone is the way, the truth, and the life. So, once more, we see that to believe in Christ is to love Christ, and to not believe in Christ is not to love Christ. Saving faith, therefore, is love for Christ.

Finally, in 2 Timothy, chapter 4, we read:

> 7 The good strife I have striven, the course I have finished, the faith I have kept. 8 Henceforth, there is laid up for me the crown of the righteousness that the Lord, the Righteous Judge, shall render to me in that day, and not only to me, but also to all those loving His appearing.
>
> (2 Tim. 4:7-8 NYLT)

Saving faith, therefore, is to lovingly long for the consummation of Christ's glorious and triumphant reign over creation (see also Matt. 24:42, 44, 25:13; Mk. 13:35; 1 Thess. 1:10, 5:6; Titus 2:13; Heb. 9:28; Rev. 16:15). It is lovingly longing for Him to be worshipped by the whole earth. it is lovingly longing for His imminent appearing, even if His return means never finishing your home remolding, or the dream vacation you have planned for next year, or retiring and enjoying your golden years, or marrying your sweetheart. Out of love for Christ, His triumphant return is much more precious than anything you desire upon this earth.

II.B.3. Supreme Delight. Saving faith is also receiving Christ as one's supreme delight. As one's supreme pleasure. As one's supreme joy. We see this, for instance, in Psalm 16:

You cause me to know the path of life;
Fulness of joys is in Your presence;
At Your right hand are pleasures forevermore!
(Ps. 16:11 NYLT)

Then look a few pages over to Psalm 21:

For You make him blessings forever;
You have made him joyful with gladness in
Your presence.

(Ps. 21:6 NYLT)

Again, in Psalm, chapter 43, we read:

And I go to the altar of God,
To God—the gladness of my joy;
And I thank You with a harp,
O God, my God.

(Ps. 43:4 NYLT)

Here again we see that saving faith is when God is the gladness of your joy. Echoing this, we read in 1 Peter 1:

[W]hom, not having seen, you love; in whom—
now not seeing yet believing—you rejoice with
joy unspeakable and glorified.
(1 Pet. 1:8 NYLT)

Notice that Peter not only describes saving faith in this verse as loving Christ and believing in Christ, but also as a rejoicing in Christ "with joy unspeakable and glorified." Finally, in John, chapter 15, we find:

"These things I have spoken to you, that My joy may remain in you and your joy may be full."
(Jn. 15:11 NYLT)

Our union with Christ is the fulness of Christ's joy abiding in us. Saving faith, therefore, is feasting upon the joy that a born-again man now has in God's presence. It is the delight he has in the eternal pleasures that he now enjoys at God's right hand. It is an insatiable but always satisfying desire for God as the source of joy unspeakable and full of glory.

II.B.4. Supreme Satisfaction. Finally, saving faith is receiving Christ as one's supreme satisfaction and rest. Peter tells us in 1 Peter 2 that:

> 1 Having put aside, then, all evil, and all deceit, and hypocrisies, and envyings, and all evil speakings, 2 as new-born babes long for the pure milk that in it you may grow, 3 if indeed you did taste that the Lord is gracious.
> (1 Pet. 2:1-3 NYLT)

Saving faith is receiving—a tasting—of Christ as completely satisfying. Or is Psalm 34:8 tells us, it is tasting and seeing that Yahweh is good. Or as Hebrews 6:5 puts it, "tast[ing] the good word of God."

Saving faith is savoring Christ as completely satisfying. We see this explicitly in several places in the Gospel of John:

• **John 4:14:** "'Whoever drinks the water I give him will never thirst. Indeed, the water I give him will become to him a spring of water welling up to eternal life.'"

- **John 6:35:** "'I am the bread of life; he who comes to Me will never hunger, and he who believes in Me will never thirst.'"

- **John 6:51:** "'I am the living bread which came down from heaven. If anyone eats of this bread, he will life forever; and the bread that I shall give is My flesh, which I shall give for the life of the world.'"

- **John 7:37-38:** "On the last day, that great day of the feast, Jesus stood and cried out, saying, 'If anyone is thirsty, let him come to Me and drink. Whoever believes in Me, as the Scripture has said, streams of living water will flow from within him.'"

Saving faith, therefore, is to be mastered, possessed, and controlled by satisfied joy in Christ that is vastly superior to all other possible joys. Christ becomes your insatiable but always satisfying addiction; your object of delight, desire, and pleasure that makes everything else look like rubbish in comparison.

II.C. All of Christ. We have seen that Scripture defines saving faith as that which : (1)receives Christ as (2) one's supreme treasure. But, now, (3) we see that saving faith is receiving all that God is in Christ. It does this in two ways.

II.C.1. First, saving faith does not merely trust Christ for salvation and stop there. No! Saving faith embraces all of God's promises to us based on that salvation. It trusts not only that we are forgiven and declared righteous through Christ, but goes even further and trusts, based on that reconciliation with God, all His other promises to us contained in Scripture:

• **2 Cor. 1:20:** "For all the promises of God in Him [Christ Jesus] are Yes, and in Him Amen, to the glory of God through us."

• **1 Cor. 3:21-23:** "21 ...For all things are yours: 22 ...or the world or life or death, or things present or things to come—all are yours! 23 And you are Christ's, and Christ is God's!"

• **2 Pet. 1:2-4:** "2 Grace and peace be multiplied to you in the knowledge of God and of Jesus our Lord, 3 as His divine power has given to us all things that pertain to life and godliness, through the knowledge of Him who called us by glory and virtue, 4 by which have been given to us exceedingly great and precious promises..."

One could spend a lifetime of lifetimes finding and clinging to the promises of God in Scripture. But among the most precious to Christians throughout the ages have been those in Romans 8:

• **Verse 28:** "And we know that all things work together for good to those who love God, to those who are the called according to His purpose."

• **Verses 31-32:** "31 What then shall we say to these things? If God is for us, who can be against us? 32 He who did not spare His own Son, but delivered Him up for us all, how shall He not with Him also freely give us all things?"

• **Verse 33:** "Who shall bring a charge against God's elect? It is God who justifies."

• **Verse 34:** "Who is he who condemns? It is Christ who died, and furthermore is also risen, who is even at the right hand of God, who also makes intercession for us."

• **Verse 35-39:** "35 Who shall separate us from the love of Christ? Shall tribulation, or distress, or persecution, or famine, or nakedness, or peril, or sword? 37 Yet in all these things we are more than conquerors through Him who loved us. 38 For I am persuaded that neither death nor life, nor angels nor principalities nor powers, nor things present nor things to come, 39 nor height nor depth, nor any other created thing, shall be able to separate us from the love of God which is in Christ Jesus our Lord."

Saving faith, therefore, claims—substantiates, foretastes, realizes—all the promises of God in Christ for future grace in full expectation that they will be fulfilled.

II.C.2. But, **secondly**, saving faith embraces all of Christ in all His roles. It doesn't accept Him as Savior without accepting Him as Lord (Rom. 10:9; 1 Jn. 3:23). Saving faith does not divide Christ but accepts Him as Creator (Jn. 1:1-3), Sustainer (Col. 1:17; Heb. 1:3), Savior (Lk. 2:11), Teacher (Jn. 13:13), Guide (Acts 16:7), Comforter (Jn. 14:18, 27; 2 Cor. 1:5)), Helper (Phil. 1:19); Friend (Jn. 15:13-15); Advocate (1 Jn. 2:1); Protector (2 Thess. 3:3); and Lord (Rom. 10:9).

II.D. To Make Much of Christ. We have seen that Scripture defines saving faith as that which : (1) receives as (2) one's supreme treasure (3) all that God is in Christ for us. But, now, (4) we see that saving faith does this to make much of Christ. We see this in Galatians:

And for me, let it not be to boast except in the cross of our Lord Jesus Messiah, through

133

which the world has been crucified to me, and
I to the world.

(Gal. 6:14 NYLT)

That is the attitude of saving faith—glorying only in Christ. As God proclaims in Jeremiah:

"But in this let the boaster boast: In understanding and knowing Me—that I am Yahweh, doing steadfast love, judgment, and righteousness in the earth. For in these I have delighted, says Yahweh."

(Jer. 9:24 NYLT)

Or as we read in 2 Corinthians 12:

7 And that I might not be exalted overmuch by the exceeding greatness of the revelations, there was given to me a thorn in the flesh, a messenger of the Adversary, that he might buffet me, that I might not be exalted overmuch. 8 Concerning this thing I did call upon the Lord three times that it might depart from me. 9 And He said to me, "My grace is sufficient for you, for My power is perfected in infirmity." Most gladly, therefore, will I rather boast in my infirmities, that the power of the Messiah may rest on me. 10 Wherefore I am well pleased in infirmities, in mistreatments, in necessities, in persecutions, in distresses—for Messiah; for whenever I am infirm, then I am powerful.

(2 Cor. 12:7-10 NYLT)

Saving faith boasts in Christ and Christ alone. A believer does not boast because God died for him because he thinks he is something special. That he was worth dying for. That he did not deserve hell. No! A believer boasts in the cross of Calvary because God has freed him to enjoy making much of Him forever. Our joy is God's greatness. Our praise is His mercy. Our rejoicing is in His grace. Because of His infinite and surpassing worth and beauty. For a genuine believer, heaven without Christ would be hell. Heaven, for a genuine believer, is not be be God, but to be with God.

III. The Sanctifying Effect of Treasuring Christ. We have seen that Scripture defines saving faith as that which receives as one's supreme treasure all that God is in Christ for them in order to make much of God. Now, finally, saving faith—in embracing the superior pleasure of Christ —kills sin. We see this in Hebrews, chapter 11:

> [24] By faith Moses, having become great, refused to be called a son of the daughter of Pharaoh, [25] having chosen rather to be afflicted with the people of God than to have sin's pleasure for a season,[26] having reckoned the reproach of the Messiah greater wealth than the treasures in Egypt, for he was fixed upon the recompense of reward.
>
> (Heb. 11:24-26 NYLT)

Verse 26 tells us that Moses valued Christ more than all the riches of Egypt, and, therefore, verse 25 tells us that he rejected the fleeting pleasures of sin. A Christian doesn't gain victory over sin by simply saying "no" to it. The allure of sin is the pleasure it appears to offer. No one ever sins out of duty. Rather, we sin because we think it will bring us greater happiness than not sinning. We lie, cheat, steal, gossip, gamble, fornicate, complain, and much more because we think it will make us happy.

Simply denying ourselves the happiness of sin sanctifies no one. Rather, as Thomas Chalmers put it, only "the expulsive power of a new affection" will sanctify a believer. Saving faith sees Christ as vastly superior to any other affection, and it is on the basis of that "expulsive power" that a born-again man loses his desire for sin. Saving faith embraces Christ as infinitely more satisfying than all the fleeting happiness that an eternity of sin could bring him. As Jim Elliot famously stated, "He is no full who gives up what he cannot keep to gain what he cannot lose." A born-again believer has counted the cost, and found Christ far superior to anything this side of eternity.

For instance, Matthew 10 we read:

> 32 "Everyone, therefore, who shall confess Me before men, I also will confess him before My Father who is in the heavens. 33 And whoever shall deny Me before men, I also will deny him before My Father who is in the heavens.
> 34 "Do not suppose that I came to put peace on the earth; I did not come to put peace, but a sword. 35 For I came to 'set a man at variance against his father, and a daughter against her mother, and a daughter-in-law against her mother-in-law,' 36 and 'the enemies of a man are those of his household.' 37 He who loves father or mother above Me is not worthy of Me, and he who loves son or daughter above Me is not worthy of Me. 38 And whoever does not receive his cross and

follow after Me is not worthy of Me. ³⁹ He who found his life shall lose it, and he who lost his life for My sake shall find it."

(Matt. 10:32-39 NYLT)

And a few chapters over in Matthew, chapter 16, we find:

²⁴ Then said Jesus to His disciples, "If anyone wills to come after Me, let him disown himself, and take up his cross, and follow Me. ²⁵ For whoever may will to save his life, shall lose it, and whoever may lose his life for My sake shall find it. ²⁶ For what is a man profited if he may gain the whole world but loses his soul? Or what shall a man give as an exchange for his soul?

(Matt. 16:24-26 NYLT)

Finally, in Luke, chapter 14, we read:

²⁵ And there were going on with Him great multitudes, and having turned, He said unto them, ²⁶ "If anyone comes unto Me and does not hate His own father and mother, and wife and children, and brothers and sisters, and, yes, even his own life, he is not able to be My disciple. ²⁷ And whoever does not bear his cross and come after Me is not able to be My disciple. ²⁸ For which of you, wanting to build a tower, does not first, having sat down, count the expense, whether he have the things for completing? ²⁹ Lest that he having laid a foundation, and not being able to finish, all

who are beholding may begin to mock him
[30] saying, 'This man began to build and was
not able to finish.' [31] Or what king going on to
engage with another king in war, does not,
having sat down, first consult if he be able with
ten thousand to meet him who with twenty
thousand is coming against him? [32] And if not,
he being yet a long way off, having sent an
embassy, he asks conditions for peace. [33] So,
then, everyone of you who does not take leave
of all that he himself has is not able to be My
disciple."

(Lk. 14:25-33 NYLT)

In other words, a born-again man—out of joy—
forsakes all else for the sake of Christ. He abandons job,
reputation, freedom, family, friends, financial security,
nation, tribe, and traditions because of the superior
pleasure of Christ. He flees pride, envy, covetousness,
anger, bitterness, lust, and all other forms of sin for the
superior pleasure of Christ. Justification is by faith alone,
but the faith the justifies is never alone. The same faith
that justifies also sanctifies because it receives as one's
superior treasure all that God is in Christ for them in order
to make much of God. Saving faith loves God supremely
and others sacrificially. Faith that still loves sin cannot be
saving faith.

Concluding Implications:

In conclusion, we have seen that Scripture defines
saving faith as that which receives as one's supreme
treasure all that God is in Christ for them in order to make
much of God and that this faith—by embracing the superior

pleasure of Christ—kills sin. As Paul tells us in Galatians 5:6—faith is love and works through love. Faith by itself is a dead faith, Jacob tells us (Jac. 2:17-19, 24, 26). Faith without love, worship, fear, and obedience is no faith at all. Examine yourself, therefore, to see if you have this faith at work in yourself. If not, repent and begin to see, seek, and savor the beauties of God in the person of Christ as the all-satisfying desire of your soul's thirst.

7 SOLA CHRISTUS

*I*n this chapter we will examine the doctrine of *Sola Christus*— that justification is in Christ alone. Or, another way of putting it, that Jesus Christ is the exclusive means of salvation. Jesus Christ isn't merely *a* lord, but *the* Lord. He isn't merely *a* god, but *the* God. He isn't merely *a* savior, but *the* Savior.

The Reformation doctrine of *Sola Christus* arose, not because the Roman Catholic Church denies Christ's deity, but because they denied His sufficiency. They maintained that justification was by Christ's atonement plus good works. Christ plus the surplus merit of Mary, Jesus' brothers, the Apostles, and a few other "super-saints." Christ plus the mediation of Mary and the other saints, which is why that apostate church offers prayers to them. Christ plus the sacraments. Christ plus the Last Rites. Christ plus the cleansing power of purgatory.

The Catholic heresy forgot that when you add something to Christ, you actually exclude Christ. Because if Christ's atonement is only 0.000000000000001% inadequate, then it is entirely, 100% inadequate. To illustrate, let's say that you owe the federal government $100 zillion, but a rich uncle gives you a check for $100 zillion so you can pay off your debt to Uncle Sam in full. But in arrogant pride you convince yourself that you still have to come up with $1 zillion yourself. So while it is theoretically better than owing the entire $100 zillion, $1 zillion remains so far beyond your capacity to pay it off that it might as well be the full $100 zillion. In effect, you have nullified that free gift from your uncle in your efforts to supplement and add to it. In the same way, any attempt to add to the sufficiency of Christ's atonement merely nullifies it and makes it of no effect (Gal. 2:21).

Though on different grounds than the cultic Roman Catholic church, most Americans today continue to undermine and deny the sufficiency and exclusivity of Christ's atonement. They reject the need for a Savior at all, believing that they are good enough to earn their way into an eternal paradise. Or, failing that attempt at self-delusion, they claim that all roads lead to heaven and that a person is free to pick and choose as many gods and saviors as they desire—whether Allah, or Budha, or the thousands of gods of Hindu, or Wakanda, and/or any other god that strikes one's fancy.

No less than during the Reformation, Christ alone—the exclusivity of the atonement of Christ—remains the most attacked truth in the world today. Since the birth of Christ 2000 years ago, it is estimated that nearly 70 million Christians have been martyred for their faith. Of that 70 million, 45 million were martyred in the 20th century alone. Despite all our advancements in science, technology, economics, health, political science, etc., the world remains quite intolerant of *Sola Christus* and, as a result, of all those who refuse to deny this precious doctrine.

I. The Need for a Savior. First, we will examine the claim by modern man that they are good enough to work their way to heaven without the need of any Savior.

I.A. Disease. In contrast, however, the Bible tells us that all of us were born unregenerate and spiritually dead. That all of us were sinners and haters of God from the moment of conception. For Scripture tells us that God created the entire universe in six, twenty-four hour calendar days (Gen. 1:1-31). In Genesis, chapter 1, we read that on the sixth day:

26 And God says, "Let Us make man in Our image, according to Our likeness, and let them rule over the fish of the sea, and over the birds of the heavens, and over the cattle, and over all the earth, and over every creeping thing that is creeping on the earth." 27 And God creates the man in His image; in the image of God He created him, a male and a female He created them. 28 And God blesses them, and God says to them, "Be fruitful, and multiply, and fill the earth, and subdue it, and rule over the fish of the sea, and over the birds of the heavens, and over every living thing that is creeping upon the earth."

(Gen. 1:26-28 NYLT)

And there was a beautiful garden there (Gen. 2:8), and Yahweh God "took the [first] man [Adam] and put him in the Garden of Eden to work it and take care of it" (vs. 15 NIV84). God created this first man Adam to never die (Gen. 2:17). God had this first man Adam name every living creature (vs. 19-20) and gave him dominion and stewardship over all of His creation (Gen. 1:26-30; 2:8-17). God gave this first man Adam Eve as the very first bride to be a suitable helpmate for him (vs. 18, 20b-23).

God walked with this first man Adam in the cool of the day (3:8). God was worshipped by this first man Adam, who was created innocent before God without shame or guilt (1:31, 2:25). And God gave this first man Adam a covenant of works that consisted of but a single commandment:

16 And Yahweh God lays a charge on the man, saying, "Of every tree of the garden eating you

143

eat; 17 and of the tree of knowledge of good
and evil, you do not eat of it, for in the day of
your eating of it—dying you die."

(Gen. 2:16-17 NYLT)

But this first man Adam and his wife Eve ate the
forbidden fruit after they "saw that the fruit of the tree was
good for food, and *pleasing* to the eye, and also *desirable*
for gaining wisdom" (Gen. 3:6; emphasis added).   And
when they did so, the Bible tells us that they inherited
eternal death (Rom. 6:23) though they continued, for a
time, to physically live (1 Tim. 5:6).

Mankind's problem, therefore, is that in the *very same
sin* that Adam sinned, all mankind sinned as well.
Romans, chapter 5, makes this explicit:

Therefore, just as sin entered the world
through one man, and death through sin, and
in this way death came to all men, because all
sinned.

(Rom. 5:12 NIV84)

We see this confirmed five other places throughout the
fifth chapter of Romans:

• **Verse 15:**   By "the one man [Adam's] offense
many died."

• **Verse 16:**   "[T]he judgment which came from one
offense resulted in condemnation."

• **Verse 17:**   "[B]y the one man [Adam's] offense
death reigned through the one."

• **Verse 18:**   "[T]hrough one man [Adam's] offense
judgment came to all men, resulting in condemnation."

• **Verse 19:** "[B]y one man [Adam's] disobedience many were made sinners."

Let me restate these five verses in reverse order to help make it clearer: (1) by the *very same* sin of our first parent Adam, all humanity was made—or imputed—to have committed the same sin as well (vs. 19); and therefore (2) all men are imputed from the moment of conception to be as guilty and unrighteous as Adam and consequently under God's rightful judgment (vs. 18) and condemnation (vs. 16, 18); which (3) resulted in both physical and spiritual death for all men (vs. 15, 17; see also 1 Cor. 15:45-49).

But not only did we inherit Adam's guilt and death as our own, but we also inherited his corrupt sin nature as our own. For the Bible tells us that you are not born as an innocent blank slate free to choice whether to be either good or bad. Rather, as a descendent of the first man Adam, you have had your sin nature from the moment of your conception. For instance, the psalmist declares, "Surely I was sinful at birth, sinful from the time my mother conceived me" (Ps. 51:5). Elsewhere we read, "Even from birth the wicked go astray; from the womb they are wayward and speak lies" (Ps. 58:3). Therefore, the problem you have is not that you commit sins, but that you are sinful. You are not a sinner because you commit sins, you commit sins because you are a sinner.

As a result, Scripture makes clear that "all have sinned and fallen short of the glory of God" (Rom. 3:23; see also 3:9) from the moment of their conception. Earlier in that same chapter we read:

9 What, then? Are we better? Not at all! For we did previously charge both Jews and Greeks with being all under sin.

10 According as it has been written:

"There is none righteous, not even one;

11 There is none who is understanding, There is none who is seeking after God.

12 All did go out of the way, Together they became unprofitable; There is none doing good, there is not even one."...

18 "There is no fear of God before their eyes."...

(Rom. 3:9-12, 18 NYLT)

You have a sin nature of inborn, spiteful rebellion against God that you cannot reform on your own. You cannot tame it. You cannot control it. You are hardwired to sin and cannot stop doing it. You have become its slave for, as Jesus said, "Most assuredly I say to you, whoever commits sin is a slave of sin" (Jn. 8:34). The Apostle Paul tells us: "Don't you know that to whom you offer yourselves to obey him as slaves, you are slaves to the one whom you obey—whether you are slaves to sin, which leads to death, or to obedience, which leads to righteousness" (Rom. 6:16 NIV84; see also 6:6, 17-18). Or as the Apostle John writes, "He who sins is of the devil, for the devil has sinned from the beginning...Whoever sins has neither seen God nor known Him" (1 Jn. 3:8, 6).

As Jeremiah tells us, "Can the Ethiopian change his skin or the leopard its spots? Neither can you do good who are accustomed to doing evil" (Jer. 13:23 NIV84). In another place, God declares through the prophet that, "The heart is deceitful above all things, and desperately wicked" (Jer. 17:9). The author of the book of Job writes, "What is man that he could become pure?" (Job 15:14; see also Job 25:4), for "who can make something pure out of what is impure? No one" (Job 14:4). Therefore, the Bible concludes that no one, "can say, 'I have made my heart pure; I am clean and without sin'" (Prov. 20:9 NIV84). Consequently, as Isaiah the prophet tells us, "We are unclean—all of us, and all our righteous acts are as menstrual rages" (NYLT).

I.B.   PROGNOSIS: Secondly, the Bible pronounces that this disease called original sin will result in eternal death, for the Apostle Paul tells us that "the wages of sin is death" (Rom. 6:23).   From birth we remain under God's holy wrath (Jn. 3:36; Eph. 2:3) and just condemnation (Jn. 3:18).   Jesus tells us that hell is an everlasting "furnace of fire in outer darkness [where you] will be wailing and gnashing [your] teeth" (Matt. 8:12, 13:42, 50, 24:51).   It is the eternal destruction of your soul (Matt. 10:28) in "fire that shall never be quenched, where '[your] worm does not die'" (Mk.. 9:44, 46, 48; see also Is. 66:24).   The Bible warns you that you "shall also drink of the wine of the wrath of God, which is poured out in full strength into...the tormented with fire and brimstone in the presence of the holy angels and in the presence of the Lamb.   And the smoke of [your] torment [will] ascend forever and ever; and [you will] have no rest day or night" (Rev. 14:10-11).

I.C.   CURE: But the Bible is also clear that God has provided us with a cure—for with as much hate as He hates you, God also loves His own elect.   For the Bible declares that God does "not want anyone to perish, but everyone to come to repentance" (2 Pet. 3:9 NIV84). He "desires all men to be saved and to come to the knowledge of the truth" (1 Tim. 2:3-4). He Himself declares that, "I have no pleasure in the death of the wicked, but that the wicked turn from his way and live" (Ezek. 33:11). Jesus said that He "came that [we] may have life, and have it abundantly, because it is not the will of His Father...that any of [you] should perish" (Jn. 10:10; Matt. 18:14).

But if God is all-loving and all-powerful and wants to save all mankind from the wages of their sins, why can He not merely forgive and forget and take us all to heaven? Because God's justice at His offended righteousness demands satisfaction. The book of Proverbs declares, for instance, that, "Whoever is justifying the wicked and condemning the righteous—even both of these are an abomination to Yahweh" (Prov. 17:15 NYLT). It is impossible, therefore, for God to simply forgive and forget your rebellion against Him without Himself being evil. Either you will be made to drink the hell of the wrath of God, or Somebody has to do it for you.

II. The Exclusivity of Christ. And that Somebody could only be the God-man Jesus Christ. Your spouse, or your parents, or your friends cannot pay the penalty of your hell for you even if they wanted to (Rom. 9:3). Neither Mohammed, the Dali Lama, the pope, the animistic witchdoctor, nor the blood of bulls and goats (Heb. 10:4) could pay the penalty of your hell for you. Rather, Scripture is clear that the only one conceivable candidate to take your place under God's wrath is the God-man Jesus Christ. Only a sacrifice that is simultaneously fully, 100% God and fully, 100% man could satisfy the immutable laws of God's nature and character, of His holiness and righteousness. We turn now to five reasons why this is so.

II.A.   First, the effectual sacrifice for sin could only be a human. In other words, because flesh and blood sinned against God, only flesh and blood could satisfy God's wrath. The blood of bulls and goats can never save a human (Heb. 10:4). The death of angels, or other spirits, or (arguendo) extraterrestrials can never save a human. The only sacrifice for a human is a human. Only the blood of a man could atone for the sins of a man.

God's perfect holiness requires perfect justice. For example, let's say you murdered someone and were facing the death sentence. But at your trial you brought before the judge your Golden Retriever as a substitute to bear your guilt and punishment. No judge in his right mind, or even one in his wrong mind, would take you up on your offer. Why? Because no animal—no matter how cute and intelligent he may be—can never adequately take the place of a human. The value of the blood of an animal is cheap, but the blood of a man is precious.

Or, to use another example, let's go back to the $100 zillion debt you owe the federal government. And you came to the IRS agent you was hounding you and said that you will pay your debt in full with 100 zillion bitcoins, or Euros, or Canadian dollars, or currency from Zimbabwe. The agent will laugh you out of his office at your audacity. Not all currency is the same. 100 zillion in U.S. dollars has to be paid back, in full, in 100 zillion U.S. dollars. There is no other adequate substitute.

It is for this reason that Jesus is called by Scripture Immanuel, which means "God with us" (Matt. 1:23). The Apostle Paul tells us that this God-man Jesus Christ, though being of the very nature and essence of God,

149

"...emptied Himself, having taken the form of a slave, having been made in the likeness of men" (Phil. 2:7 NYLT). Even though He was very God of very God, Scripture declares that Jesus "did not live to please Himself" (Rom. 15:2). Instead, He became the submissive and obedient love-slave of His Father, telling us, "'I have come down from heaven, not to do My own will but the will of Him who sent Me'" (Jn. 6:28).

And this God-man Jesus Christ is so fearfully awesome and unique (i.e., holy) in His moral excellencies and divine power that it can barely be grasped or described, yet He subjected Himself to the humility of being born of a virgin and taking on the flesh and bones of His mere creatures. He became liable to get sick as we get sick; to get headaches as we get headaches; to be lonely as we get lonely (Is. 53:3); to grow weary and hungry as we grow weary and hungry (Matt. 4:2; Lk. 4:2; Jn. 4:6-7, 19:28). He was obedient to His parents (Lk. 2:51; Jn. 19:25-27); grieved over death as we grieve (Jn. 11:33, 35, 38), and was tempted in every way as we are tempted, though He did not sin (Heb. 2:18, 4:15). In short, "in all things He was made to be like us" (Heb. 2:17).

Why? Because God had to "sen[d] His own Son in the likeness of sinful flesh [in order to] condemn sin in the flesh" (Rom. 8:3). Or as the author of Hebrews explains:

> [14] Seeing, then, the children have partaken of flesh and blood, He Himself also in like manner did take part of the same, that through death He might destroy him having the power of death—that is, the devil—[15] and might deliver those who through fear of death throughout all their life were subjects to bondage.

(Heb. 2:14-15 NYLT)

In Romans, chapter 5, we find that the first man Adam prefigured (vs. 14) the coming second Adam—the God-man Jesus Christ:

> 12 Because of this, even as through one man sin entered into the world, and through sin—death, and thus to all men death passed through, for that all sinned...15 But the gracious gift is not as the offense. For if by the trespass of the one many died, much more did the grace of God, and the free gift in grace of the one Man Jesus Christ, abound to many. 16 And the free gift is not through the one who did sin. For judgment of that one resulted in condemnation, but the gracious gift which came from many offenses resulted in a declaration of "Righteous." 17 For if by the offense of the one death reigned through the one, much more those who are receiving the abundance of grace and of the free gift of righteousness shall reign in life through the One—Jesus Christ. 18 So, then, as through one offense condemnation came to all men, so also through one act of righteousness justification of life came to all men. 19 For as through the disobedience of the one man, many were appointed sinners, so also through the obedience of the One shall many be appointed righteous.
>
> (Rom. 5:12, 15-19 NYLT)

In Adam's sin all mankind sinned as well and inherited his guilt, condemnation, and eternal death. Therefore, only a Second Adam could redeem Adam's helpless race. Only one born in the flesh could serve as our kinsman redeemer (Is. 59:20) to redeem us from the wrath of God. Consequently, our atonement could only be made by the God-man Jesus Christ because, since human flesh and blood sinned against God, only human flesh and blood could satisfy God's wrath.

II.B.   The **second** reason only the God-man Jesus Christ could satisfy the immutable laws of God's nature and character, of His holiness and righteousness is because, in order to be an effectual sacrifice for sin, the sacrifice must be perfect. Why? Because our substitute needs to succeed where we failed by perfectly fulfilling the law of God.   Our failure to perfectly fulfill God's commandments has brought us under the penalty of eternal hell. We are all guilty many, many times over before the tribunal of God.

And it is a logical and biblical impossibility that a person under the punishment of eternal death—which all of us are from the moment of conception—could also pay the punishment of eternal death for someone else. A guilty man under the rightful punishment of death cannot also pay the rightful punishment of death for another guilty man. The reason is simple—for if your punishment is death, and you can only die once, you can logically only pay for your own crime and not for another's.

Likewise, all mankind stands under the sentence of eternal hell; an infinity of suffering which they will never be able to pay off. Their eternal punishment is eternal because it cannot be satisfied. So it is a logical impossibility that a guilty man who has an eternal debt of sin to pay for in an infinite hell could ever pay it for himself and then for another also. A finite person can never satisfy an infinite punishment for himself, much less for someone else.

Therefore, only a perfect, sinless, innocent sacrifice in human flesh (Heb. 4:15, 9:14) not already under eternal judgment could pay someone else's eternal judgment. Only a perfect, sinless, innocent sacrifice in human flesh who was not in need of a Savior Himself could serve as the Savior for the rest of humanity. Consequently, only a perfect, sinless, innocent sacrifice in human flesh that perfectly fulfilled all the law of God could serve as the atoning sacrifice for mankind's sins. And since no man in history ever satisfied that requirement, only the pure and holy God in human flesh could.

This is why our Savior has to be a God-man, because only a perfect God can perfectly satisfy the perfect law of God. Only a perfect God can perfectly love HImself supremely and thereby satisfy the perfect law of God. Only a perfect God can perfectly love others as Himself and thereby satisfy the perfect law of God. Only a perfect God cannot sin. And therefore only a perfect God can perfectly atone for sin.

This is why Jesus tells us that He did not come "to destroy the Law or the Prophets," "but to fulfill" them (Matt. 5:17). He came to render to God the Father the perfect obedience we never could in order to "fulfill all righteousness" (Matt. 3:15). In Luke, chapter 24, we find Jesus telling HIs disciples after His resurrection that:

> 44 "These are the words which I spoke to you while I was still with you, that all things must be fulfilled which were written in the Law of Moses and the Prophets and the Psalms

concerning Me." [45] And He opened their understanding, that they might comprehend the Scriptures.

> (Lk. 24:44-45; see also vs. 25-27).

Therefore, the God-man Jesus Christ is our exclusive Savior because only One who is fully, 100% God could perfectly fulfilled the law of God.

II.C.   **Third**, the effectual sacrifice for sin could only be God in human flesh who became a perfect and merciful High Priest. The author of Hebrews tells us:

> For it was becoming to Him, because of whom are the things and through whom are the all things, in bringing many sons to glory, to make the initiator of their salvation perfect through sufferings.
>
> (Heb. 2:10 NYLT)

And a few chapters later in Hebrews we read:

> through being a Son, He learned obedience by the things which He suffered.
>
> (Heb. 5:8 NYLT)

Is the Bible saying that Christ was imperfect and had to be perfected?   That He was disobedient and had to learn obedience? That is not only dubious but also blasphemous in light of other passages in the book of Hebrews alone.   Hebrews 4:15, for instance, declares emphatically that Jesus "was in all points tempted as we are, yet without sin." And in Hebrews 9:14 the author tells us that Christ was "without spot."

So what do these verses mean when they tell us that Christ had to be made perfect through learning obedience by the things He suffered (Heb. 2:10, 5:8)? Not that the God-man Jesus Christ had not been previously imperfect or disobedient, but rather that it was through suffering that His untested yet perfect obedience to God the Father was tested and found to remain perfect. Our first man Adam's obedience to God was tested in the Garden of Eden and he failed miserably, imputing all his progeny with his sin and condemnation. In contrast, however, our Second Adam Jesus Christ passed the test and, having been found perfect (Heb. 2:10), we are told that "...He became the cause of age-enduring salvation to all those obeying Him" (Heb. 5:9 NYLT). He alone is qualified to serve as the Second Adam, so that by faith in Him our union with the first man Adam is severed as we are united with—and eternally live through—the righteousness of the Second Adam Jesus Christ.

But not only did Christ succeed where Adam failed, but, because of His sufferings and temptations, He is able to serve as a merciful High Priest. We also see this in Hebrews, chapter 2:

> [17] Therefore, it behoved Him to be made like His brethren in all things, that He might become a merciful and steadfast Chief Priest in the things of God, to make propitiation for the sins of the people. [18] For in that He suffered, Himself being tempted, He is able to help those who are tempted.
>
> (Heb. 2:17-18 NYLT)

Notice the language of verse 17: "it *behoved* Him to be make like His brethren in all things" (emphasis added). It behoved Him. It was necessary. It was obligatory. The original Greek is even stronger: "in all things He *was morally indebted* to be made like His brethren." Why? Why was is morally necessary that Christ be made like His brethren? We see the answer in verse 18: "For in that He suffered, Himself being tempted, He is able to help those who are tempted." Or as verse 17 tells us—Christ was morally indebted to be made like His brethren in all things *so that* He might be a merciful and faithful Chief Priest.

It was necessary, in the wisdom and goodness of God the Father, that our Savior could only be a merciful High Priest. A common expression these days is that one cannot judge another until they have walked a mile in their shoes. We love to defend ourselves by saying, "Don't judge me because you don't know..." Or "you can't criticize me because you haven't experience..." HR departments will often stress the difference between sympathy with empathy. Sympathy, they argue, is akin to pity. It says to someone hurting, "I care about you." In contrast, someone who empathizes with another says, "I'm hurting with you." Another way of putting it is that empathy is our ability to feel what someone else feels while sympathy is our relief in not experiencing the same hurt.

The point of this passage from Hebrews, however, is that we cannot say to God that He doesn't understand. That He doesn't empathize. That He doesn't really know our situation because He hasn't experienced it. No! We have a merciful, empathetic High Priest in the God-Man Jesus Christ who experienced suffering and temptation just as we do and so He is able to not only understand our pain and doubts but give us the appropriate, well-timed grace. He is not a remote, aloof God who doesn't understand the hardships of His creation. He is not an angelic being who doesn't understand the trials of humanity. He is not a extraterrestrial indifferent to our plight. No! It is precisely because He is fully, 100% God and fully, 100% man that He is able to serve as our HIgh Priest and give us the aid of His grace when we need it, in the measure that we need it (Heb. 2:16, 18).

But not only did He suffer and was tempted, He did so without sinning. Therefore, as a prefect, sinless High Priest, He is able to approach the throne of God the Father to make unceasing intercession on our behalf (Rom. 8:34; 1 Tim. 2:5; Heb. 7:25, 9:24; 1 Jn. 2:1). Neither Mary, nor the Apostles, nor Mohammed, the Dali Lama, the pope, the animistic witchdoctor, nor an animal sacrifice can fulfill this role of High Priest because, due to their sins, they cannot enter into the throne room of heaven. Nor, due to their mortality, can they serve as a living, eternal High Priest. Nor do they have any grace, power, or righteousness with which to bestow on us.

Therefore, only the God-man Jesus Christ—innocent and righteous, eternal and holy, tempted yet sinless—can fulfill the role of a merciful and steadfast Chief Priest, without which there could be no atonement for sins.

II.D.   Fourth, the effectual sacrifice for sin could only be God in human flesh whose shed blood was of sufficient quality to serve as an atonement for sin. Our sin against an eternal God demands an eternal damnation. Our sin against an infinite God demands an infinite retribution. Our sin against a God unfathomable in His holiness and righteousness demands a vengeance and wrath equally unfathomable. Therefore, only a sacrifice that was fully God could fully satisfy the eternal, infinite, unfathomable hell of God's wrath for just one individual, much less for the millions who put their trust in Him.

The Bible makes this explicitly clear in John, chapter
3:

> [14] "And as Moses lifted up the serpent in the
> wilderness, so it *behoves* the Son of Man to
> be lifted up, [15] *in order that* everyone who is
> believing in Him may not perish, but may have
> life age-enduring. [16] For God so agaped the
> world, that His Son—the only begotten—He
> gave, that everyone who is believing in Him
> may not perish but may have life age-
> enduring...
> [18] "He who is believing in Him is not judged,
> but he who is not believing has been judged
> already, because he has not believed in the
> name of the only begotten Son of God...
> [36] "He who is believing in the Son, has life
> age-enduring; and he who is not believing the
> Son, shall not see life, but the wrath of God
> remains upon him."
> (Jn. 3:14-16, 18, 36 NYLT; emphasis added)

Catch the connection there in verses 14 and 15: the
sacrifice of the God-man Jesus Christ is *necessary as the
only means* for sinful man to be redeemed and reconciled
to God.

Then in Hebrews, chapter 9, we read:

> [11] And Messiah having come—Chief Priest of
> the coming good things, through the greater
> and more perfect Tent not made with hands,
> that is, not of this creation, [12] neither through
> blood of goats and calves, but through His
> own blood He entered into the Holies once for

all, having obtained age-enduring redemption.
13 For if the blood of bulls and goats and ashes of a heifer, sprinkling those defiled, sanctified to the purifying of the flesh, 14 how much more shall the blood of the Messiah—who through the age-enduring Spirit did offer Himself unblemished to God—purify your conscience from dead works to serve the living God?...
23 It is necessary, therefore, for the pattern of the things in the heavens to be purified with these, and the heavenlies themselves with better sacrifices than these.   24 For the Messiah did not enter into holies made with hands—figures of the true—but into the heaven itself, now to appear in the presence of God for us.

(Heb. 9:11-14, 23-24 NYLT)

In other words, because the God-man Jesus Christ was fully God, He alone was able to enter into heaven with the better sacrifice of His own blood in order to purify us from all sin and thereby enable us to live together with Him in the presence of God the Father. For the Bible tells us that, "without the shedding of blood there is no forgiveness" of sins (Heb. 9:22 NIV84), but then it also tells us that "it is impossible for the blood of bulls and goats to take away sins" (Heb. 10:4 NIV84). The blood of mere mortals alone cannot atone for sin, but rather Hebrews 10:10 tells us that "we have been made holy [only] through the sacrifice of the body of Jesus Christ once for all" (Heb. NIV84).

II.E.   The **fifth** and **final** reason is that the effectual sacrifice for sin could only be God in human flesh who was raised from the dead with the same body He had lived and died in, but only after it had been transformed into an incorruptible, imperishable, indestructible resurrected body. Because through the first man Adam we inherited a mortal body, now through the second Adam Jesus Christ we inherit an immortal body,

We see this explicitly in 1 Corinthians, chapter 15:

> [21] For since through *one* man came death, also through *one* Man came the resurrection of the dead. [22] For even as in Adam all die, so also in the Messiah shall all be made alive...
>
> [42] So also is the resurrection of the dead: it is sown in corruption, it is raised in incorruption; [43] it is sown in dishonor, it is raised in glory; it is sown in weakness, it is raised in power; [44] it is sown a natural body, it is raised a spiritual body. There is a natural body, and there is a spiritual body. [45] So also it has been written, "The first man Adam became a living creature." The last Adam is a life-giving spirit.
>
> [46] But that which is spiritual is not first, but that which was natural, afterwards that which is spiritual. [47] The first man is out of the earth, earthy; the second Man is the Lord out of heaven. [48] As is the earthy, such are also the earthy; and as is the heavenly, such are also the heavenly—[49] and, according as we did bear the image of the earthy, we shall bear also the image of the heavenly.
>
> (1 Cor. 15:21-22, 42-49 NYLT)

In other words, only a perfect, sinless God-man could defeat death. For the Bible tells us that the wages of sin is death—physical and eternal (Rom. 6:23). The grave has a rightful claim on every single one of us because we have all sinned and fallen short of the glory of God (Rom. 3:23). The only Person, therefore, who has ever lived who death had no claim on is the sinless God-man Jesus Christ. If God had not take on flesh and blood to live a perfectly holy and righteous life in our stead, our bodies would forever remain in the grave. And if there is no resurrection from the dead, then the Bible tells us that our "faith is futile [and we] are still in []our sins!" (1 Cor. 15:17).

But thanks be to God that the grave could not hold the God-man Jesus Christ! Justice required—nay, demanded —that the grave spit out the prefect, sinless God-man! The Apostle Paul tells us that the Holy Spirt "justified" (NKJV) or "vindicated" (ESV) Jesus as righteous by raising Him from His wrongful imprisonment in the grave (1 Tim. 3:16). Having disarmed the grave, Christ made a public spectacle of it—leading death as His prisoner in a triumphant procession (Col. 2:15).

The 15th chapter of 1 Corinthians triumphantly concludes:

> [50] And this I say, brethren, that flesh and blood is not able to inherit the kingdom of God, nor does corruption inherit incorruption. [51] Behold! —I tell you an initiation mystery: we indeed shall not all sleep, and we all shall be changed —[52] in a moment, in the twinkling of an eye, at the last trumpet. For it shall sound, and the dead shall be raised incorruptible, and we shall be changed. [53] For it behoves this corruptible to put on incorruption, and this mortal to put on immortality. [54] And when this corruptible may have put on incorruption, and

this mortal may have put on immortality, then shall be brought to pass the word that has been written, "Death was swallowed up to victory!" 55 "Where, O Death, is your sting? Where, O Hades, is your victory?" 56 The sting of the death is sin, and the power of sin is the law. 57 And to God be thanks—to Him who is giving us the victory through our Lord Jesus Messiah. 58 So that, my agaped brethren, become firmly established, unmovable, abounding in the work of the Lord at all times, knowing that your labour in the Lord is not vain.

(1 Cor. 15:50-58 NYLT)

This is the hope of those of us who have been united by faith with the Second Adam Jesus Christ. Where, O Death, is your sting?! And where, O Hades, is your victory?! Therefore, our labor, our patience, our hope in the Lord is not in vain for we shall inherit eternal life!

Concluding Implications:

In conclusion, we have seen that the Scriptures provide five reasons why the immutable laws of God's nature and character, of His holiness and righteousness necessitate that forgiveness of sins and reconciliation with God the Father is only possible through the sacrificial death of His one and only begotten Son Jesus Christ:

(1) The sacrifice could only be God in human flesh because, since human flesh and blood sinned against God, only human flesh and blood could satisfy God's wrath;

162

(2) The sacrifice could only be God in human flesh who was innocent because He perfectly fulfilled the law of God;

(3) The sacrifice could only be God in human flesh who became a perfect and merciful High Priest;

(4) The sacrifice could only be God in human flesh whose shed blood was of sufficient quality to serve as an atonement for sin; and

(5) The sacrifice could only be God in human flesh because, through the resurrected second Adam Jesus Christ, we inherit an immortal body and are freed from the curse of sin.

If the God-man Jesus Christ were not the exclusive means of salvation, God the Father would be a cruel monster not worth one trillisecond of your worship. Those who believe that all religions are equally true, equally valid, and equally lead to God often argue that if Jesus Christ is the one and only means of salvation, then God must be cruel. The opposite, however, is true. For if all religions lead to God, why then did God kill His one and only begotten Son? If God didn't have to sacrifice His Son to save a fallen humanity but rather did so out of sadistic choice, He would be a cruel child-molester of cosmic proportions. If Allah, Buddha, Wakanda, or any run-of-the-mill religion could save you from an eternity in hell, then God is evil personified who needlessly humiliated and killed His own Son. Unless, of course, Christianity is false, which then destroys the modern premise that all religions are equally true, which then means Christianity must be the only true religion because it is the only one that fully and completely satisfies the immutable laws of God's nature and character, of His holiness and righteousness.

This is why the Bible declares that, "Nor is there salvation in any other, for there is no other name under heaven given among men by which we must be saved" (Acts 4:12).   As Jesus Himself made clear, He alone is the only way, the only truth, and the only life, and absolutely no one comes to God the Father except through Him (Jn. 14:6).   In numerous other places the Bible describes Jesus as the one, only, and final sacrifice for sins, of which no other can either be offered to or accepted by God (Heb. 7:27; see also Rom. 6:10; 1 Pet. 3:18). Finally, Philippians, chapter 2, tells us that:

> 9 Therefore, also, God did highly exalt Him, and gave to Him the name that is above every name, 10 that at the name of Jesus every knee may bow—of heavenlies, and earthlies, and what are under the earth—11 and every tongue may confess that Jesus Messiah is Lord, to the glory of God the Father.
>
> (Phil. 2:9-11 NYLT)

Salvation is only possible through the God-man Jesus Christ because only a perfect, sinless person who was both fully, 100% God and fully, 100% man could perfectly satisfy God's perfect justice.   Not Allah, or Buddha, or Wakanda, or any other so-called "god."   Rather, forgiveness of sins and peace with God is only possible through the imputation of Christ's blood and righteousness alone that comes through repentance and faith (Jn. 1:12, 3:17-18, 5:24, 6:40, 47, 11:25-26; Acts 16:31; Rom. 10:13; Heb. 9:26, 28).   Justification is through Christ and Christ alone! *Sola Christus*!

8 SOLA DEO GLORIA

*I*n this final chapter we will examine the fifth and remaining doctrine of *Sola Deo Gloria*—that justification is for God's glory alone. But to do so we must answer three fundamental questions: (1) what do we mean by God's glory? (2) how is justification to God's glory? and (3) how is God not an egomaniac?

1. The Weight of Glory. First, what do we mean by God's glory? How do we define the glory of God? This is a question far easier to ask than to answer. It is akin to trying to define beauty. My dictionary defines beauty as the combination of qualities that pleases the senses. Though that isn't a bad definition of the word, the application of the definition is much harder.

For instance, if you had no idea what a football was you would, after I described it to you, be able to identify a football anywhere in the world. However, if I said that the sunset was beautiful, or the symphony was beautiful, or sailing on the ocean is beautiful, you would have no idea what I was talking about other than the fact that it pleased me. But you wouldn't know why it pleased me. I would then have to explain in more detail what it was about those things that pleased my emotional, intellectual, and/or physical senses.

Similarly, when it comes to glory—you know it when you see it. And you may never be able to fully explain why it is glorious, but you know beyond a shadow of a doubt that it is. And you certainly may not be able to define the term *glory*. Even my dictionary failed to come up with a workable definition of glory. In fact, the third definition it offered was that glory was something beautiful.

165

But while difficult, we are going to make an attempt from Scripture to define what is the glory of God. In Isaiah, chapter 6, we find one of the most fundamental passages to understanding God's glory:

> [1] In the year of the death of King Uzziah I see Adonai sitting on a throne, high and lifted up, and the train *of His robe* is filling the temple. [2] Seraphs are standing above it, each one has six wings: with two each covers its face, and with two each covers its feet, and with two each flies. [3] And this one has called unto that, and has said, "Holy, Holy, Holy, is Yahweh Sabaoth! All the earth is full of His glory!
>
> (Is. 6:1-3 NYLT)

In verse three the word *holy* is used three times, which is a Hebrew literary device to emphasis the weightiness and magnitude of the word. Here the seraphim thrice cried out, "Holy, holy, holy" (vs. 3) to stress the infinite and unsurpassed holiness of Yahweh Sabaoth. God's holiness is to the superlative degree—His holiness is perfect, unable to be improved upon, and shared by no rival.

But look at the end of verse three. One would logically assume that the seraphim will conclude their refrain by crying out, "all the earth is full of His *holiness*!" But they don't. Rather, they revel in the fact that, "all the earth is full of His *glory*!" Why? Are the terms *holiness* and *glory* the same and used here interchangeably? Or are they different and, if so, why use both of them in this passage?

Sefaria, the Hebrew word for *holiness*, doesn't necessarily mean good or pure, though, depending on the context, that may be implied. Rather, it literally means to *separate* or *set apart*. When applied to God, therefore, *holiness* refers to Yahweh's uniqueness. His utter set-apartness from anything or anyone else. It is Yahweh's intrinsic value and worth in being God; the essential or innate splendor and beauty of His being—His attributes, character, and virtues. In contrast, the Hebrew word for *glory* is *kabod*, which literally means *weight*. It refers to the radiance or outward display of God's intrinsic and essential value and beauty, like rays of light emanating from the sun.

So, for example, the holiness—or utter set-apartness—of God as Creator is glorified—or displayed—in every act of His creative power. The holiness—or utter set-apartness—of God's mercy and grace is glorified—or manifested—in every act of pity and goodness He bestows on mankind. The holiness—or utter set-apartness—of God's sovereignty is glorified—or demonstrated—in every act of Providence in human history.

God's glory, therefore, is His holiness displayed. And this weight of God's beautiful holiness, this magnitude of His utter set-apartness, this majesty of His absolute uniqueness, is displayed for men to grasp at and seek to understand as it produces in them worship, fear, love, and obedience.

In Romans, chapter 1, we read:

> [18] For the wrath of God is revealed from heaven upon all impiousness and unrighteousness of men, who are holding down the truth in unrighteousness, [19] because that which is known of God is manifest among them, for God did manifest it to them. [20] For from the creation of the world the invisible things of Him are plainly seen, being understood by the things made

—both His eternal power and Godhead—so
that they are inexcusable.

(Rom. 1:18-20 NYLT)

Look at verses 19 and 20 again: What may be known
of God is obvious to mankind for He has clearly shown to
them His invisible attributes, eternal power, and Godhead
in the things that are made. In other words, everything in
creation glorifies—or declares—the holiness—or utter set-
apartness—of God, so that all men everywhere are without
excuse for their behavior (Rom. 1:20, 2:10). God's glory,
therefore, is the display or manifestation of His holiness in
everything He does.

And this is the purpose for which God created the
universe—to magnify His glory. Earth is 8,077 miles in
diameter. In contrast, the sun, the largest object in our
solar system, is 869,919 miles in diameter. That's 109
times the diameter of the earth, and 1 million earth-size
planets can fit inside our sun. The distance between the
earth and the sun is 93 million miles, with the distance
between the earth and the farthest planet Neptune is 3
billion miles. In contrast, the estimated size of our solar
system is 12 trillion miles in diameter. In contrast to that,
the observable universe is a whopping 547 trillion (93 light
years) across. That means that the known universe is one
octillion (1,000, 000, 000, 000, 000, 000, 000, 000, 000)
larger than a human being.

The point of all creation is to make us feel small, to put
mankind in our place. All of creation screams at us
continually that, "You are not the point!" Rather, the point
of the entire creation is not man's glory but God's. This is
why Scripture declares, "The heavens declare the glory of
God, and the firmament shows His handiwork" (Ps. 19:1).
Or as King David proclaims: "O Yahweh, our Adonai, how

majestic is Your name in all the earth! Who sets Your glory above the heavens!" (Ps. 8:1 NYLT). And a few verses later the he rejoices, "O Yahweh, our Adonai, how majestic is Your name in all the earth!" (Ps. 8:9 NYLT). Several chapters later the Bible declares, "High above the nations is Yahweh, above the heavens is His glory!" (Ps. 113:4 NYLT). And Psalm 50:6 proclaims, "the heavens declare His righteousness!" (ESV). All of creation glorifies—or displays—the holiness—or utter set-apartness—of God. He alone is God, and He created all things—visible and invisible—just to show how beautiful He really is. Therefore we cry out with the psalmist, "Not unto us, O Yahweh, not unto us, but to Your name give glory, for Your steadfast love, and for Your truth!" (Ps. 115:1 NYLT).

II. The Glory of Grace. Now that we know what we mean by God's glory, we must now turn to the second question: how is justification for God's glory? The answer is simple: because it is all—from eternity past to eternity future—of God.

II.A. Predestination. We read in Ephesians, chapter 1, that:

> 3 Blessed is the God and Father of our Lord Jesus Messiah, who blessed us with every spiritual blessing in the heavenlies in Messiah, 4 just as He did choose us in Him before the foundation of the world, for our being holy and unblemished before Him in agape,5 having predestined us to the adoption of sons through Jesus Messiah to Himself, according to the good pleasure of His will, 6 to the praise of the glory of His grace, in which He did make us

accepted in the Agaped, [7] in whom we have redemption through His blood, the remission of the trespasses, according to the riches of His grace, [8] which He abounded toward us in all wisdom and prudence, [9] having made known to us the initiation mystery of His will, according to His good pleasure that He purposed in Himself,

[10] that in the stewardship of the fulness of the times, to bring into one the whole in the Messiah, both the things in the heavens and the things upon the earth—in Him!

[11] In whom also we did obtain an inheritance, being predestined according to the purpose of Him who is working all things according to the counsel of His will, [12] for our being to the praise of His glory, even those who did first hope in the Messiah, [13] in whom you also, having heard the word of the truth—the gospel of your salvation; in whom also having believed, you were sealed with the Holy Spirit of the promise, [14] who is an earnest of our inheritance until the redemption of the acquired possession—to the praise of His glory!

(Eph. 1:3-14 NYLT)

We could spend a month of Sundays on these twelve verses alone, but let me highlight just a few things:

- **Verse 4:** God chose who would believe in Him before the foundation of the world.
- **Verse 5:** God predestined those believers according to His good will.

- **Verse 6:** And God so chose and predestined in order to elicit praise of the glory—or display—of His grace.
- **Verse 7:** We have been redeemed to glorify—or display or demonstrate—the riches of His grace.
- **Verse 11:** We were predestined according to His sovereign electing will so that:
- **Verse 12:** Those who first trusted in Christ should be to the praise of His glory,
- **Verses 13-14:** And that those who later trusted in Christ should also be to the praise of His glory.

To recap: verses 4, 5, and 11 tell us that those of us who believe were predestined before the foundation of the world, and verses 6, 7, and 12-14 explain that the reason believers were predestined—or chosen—is to the praise of God's glory.

And God's sovereign choice—or election or predestination—of who He would save is owing to nothing whatsoever in an individual. God's election is completely and entirely sovereign, free, and unconditional. You can never become good enough or righteous enough for God to predestine you. In fact, as Ephesians 1:4-5 and 11 just told us, we were chosen by God before we were conceived or even the first molecule in the universe was created. There is nothing we did to contribute to our election.

In Romans 9, the Apostle Paul clearly establishes this:

- **Verse 11:** God's electing purpose—established before we were born and have done any good or evil—will stand.
- **Verse 12:** Salvation is "not of works but of Him who calls."

- **Verse 16:** "So then it is not of him who wills, nor of him who runs, but of God who shows mercy."
- **Verse 18:** "Therefore [God] has mercy on whom He wills, and whom He wills He hardens."

In fact, in Romans 9 Paul tells us that God predestines both those who will believe and those who will not believe:

> 6 And it is not possible that the word of God has failed. For not all who are of Israel are these Israel, 7 nor because they are seed of Abraham are all children, but, "In Isaac shall your seed be called." 8 That is, the children of the flesh, these are not children of God; but the children of the promise are reckoned as seed. 9 For the word of promise is this: "According to this time I will come, and there shall be a son to Sarah."
>
> (Ro. 9:6-9 NYLT)

Look at the first person mentioned in this passage who was predestined by God—Abraham. God called Abraham, a moon-worshipper living in the Ur of the Chaldeans, and gave him a promise. Genesis, chapter 12, begins:

> 1 And Yahweh says unto Abram, "Go from your land, and from your family, and from the house of your father, unto the land which I show you. 2 And I make you become a great nation, and bless you, and make your name great; and you be a blessing. 3 And I bless those blessing you, and he who is disesteeming you I curse, and blessed in you have been all families of the ground."

(Gen. 12:1-3 NYLT)

God chose—or elected or predestined—Abraham. Not Abraham's father Terah. Not Abraham's brothers Nabor and Haran. Not Abraham's nephew Lot. But Abraham—owing to nothing whatsoever in Abraham but solely as a result of God's completely and entirely sovereign, free, and unconditional election.

Then the second person who Paul tells us in Romans 9 was predestined by God was Isaac. Not Ishmael, Isaac's older half-brother, but Isaac. And Genesis, chapter 17, tells us that God declared His predestination of Isaac an entire year before he was born:

> 18 And Abraham says unto God, "O that Ishmael may live before You!" 19 And God says, "Sarah your wife is certainly bearing a son to you, and you has called his name Isaac, and I have established My covenant with him, for a covenant age-enduring, to his seed after him. 20 As to Ishmael, I have heard you. Behold!—I have blessed him, and made him fruitful, and multiplied him very exceedingly. Twelve princes he begets, and I have made him become a great nation. 21 And My covenant I establish with Isaac, whom Sarah bears to you at this appointed time in the next year."
>
> (Gen. 17:18-21 NYTL)

Before Isaac was born or had done anything good or evil (Rom. 9:11), God choose him over his brother Ismael —owing to nothing whatsoever in Isaac but solely as a result of God's completely and entirely sovereign, free, and unconditional election.

The third person who Paul tells us in Romans 9 was predestined by God was Jacob:

> 10 And not only so, but also Rebecca, having conceived by one—Isaac our father—11 (for they being not yet born, neither having done anything good or evil, that according to the electing purpose of God might remain; not of works, but of Him who is calling)— 12 it was said to her, "The greater shall serve the less;' 13 according as it has been written, "Jacob I loved, and Esau I hated."
>
> (Rom. 9:10-13 NYLT)

In this passage we are told that while Rebecca, Isaac's wife, was pregnant with twins, God predestined one over the other. They had the same father. They had the same mother. And neither had yet done anything good or evil (vs. 11). But God loved Jacob and hated Esau (vs. 13)—owing to nothing whatsoever in either twin but solely as a result of God's completely and entirely sovereign, free, and unconditional election.

The fourth and final person who Paul tells us in Romans 9 was predestined by God was Pharaoh:

> 17 For the Holy Writing says to Pharaoh, "For this very thing I did raise you up, that I might show in you My power, and that My name might be declared in all the land." 18 So, then, to whom He wills, He has mercy, and to whom He wills, He hardens.
>
> (Rom. 9:17-18 NYLT)

God raised up Pharaoh and hardened his heart in order to display His power and gain the glory. Even before Moses had stepped foot in Egypt as God's appointed messenger to deliver the Israelites out of slavery, God had told him that He would harden Pharaoh's heart "so that he will not let the people go" (Ex. 4:21). God predestined Pharaoh for destruction—owing to nothing whatsoever in Pharaoh but solely as a result of God's completely and entirely sovereign, free, and unconditional election. "Yahweh has worked for Himself, and also the wicked for the day of evil" (Prov. 16:4 NYLT).

Therefore, God's choosing—or election or predestination—is the free act of the sovereign God in which from eternity past (Eph. 1:4, 11), for reasons only known to Himself (Matt. 11:27), and apart from any foreseen faith and/or goodness found in them (Rom. 8:29-30, 9:11; 2 Tim. 1:9), He graciously chose from among the fallen mankind a people unto salvation that they might be conformed to Christ's image (Eph. 4:13). In ages past, before the creation of the world and anyone was born or had done a single deed, whether good or bad, God sovereignly, freely, and unconditionally chose from among a humanity—blind, hardened, and dead in their sinful nature—those who would receive the Gospel and thereby be undeservedly saved for all eternity and those who would remain a rebel against God and thereby be deservedly damned for all eternity.

Why?:

> [19] You will say to me then, "Why does He yet find fault? For who has resisted His counsel?" [20] O man, indeed, who are you that are answering against God? Shall the thing

formed say to Him who formed it, "Why did You make me thus?" 21 Has not the potter authority over the clay, to out of the same lump make the one vessel to honor and the one to dishonor? 22 And if God, willing to show His wrath and to make known His power, did endure, in much long-tempering, vessels of wrath fitted for destruction, 23 and that He might make known the riches of His glory on vessels of mercy, that He prepared beforehand for glory, 24 whom also He did call —us—not only out of Jews, but also out of the ethnic groups.

(Rom. 9:19-24 NYLT)

God exercises His completely and entirely sovereign, free, and unconditional election to maximize His own glory by removing any grounds for boasting in those who are saved. You do not make yourself a Christian, but rather God makes you a Christian because He choose to do so before time even began. You are not elect by God because He foresaw that you would believe; rather, you believe because you are the elect of God. Therefore, to God alone belongs the glory.

II.B. All is a Gift. Not only is our predestination owing to God and God alone, but all of salvation—from start to finish—is a gracious gift of God:

28 And we have known that to those loving God all things do work together for good, to those who are called according to purpose. 29 Because whom He did foreknow, He also predestined to be conformed to the image of

> His Son, that He might be the firstborn among many brethren. [30] And whom He did predestine, these also He called; and whom He called, these also He declared righteous; and whom He declared righteous, these also He glorified.
>
> (Rom. 8:28-30 NYLT)

Look with me at this unbreakable chain of God's completely and entirely sovereign, free, and unconditional electing will: those whom God foreknew, He predestines, then He calls them, then He justifies them, and then He glorifies them! Notice that this unbreakable chain of God's sovereign, electing love is all about God. He initiated it. He implemented it. He obtained it. He applies it. He guarantees it. And He will complete it until the very end. The only thing we contribute to our salvation is our sin.

And while we are commanded to, and remain responsible for, repenting and believing the Gospel, repentance and faith are but gifts of God's sovereign, electing will.

II.B.1. Faith is a Gift. For instance, Scripture commands us to believe in the Lord Jesus Christ and we will be saved (Rom. 16:31). But then over and over again in the New Testament we are told that we cannot believe on our own but that it must be a gift from God. Matthew 16, for example, reads:

> [13] And Jesus, having come to the parts of Caesarea Philippi, was asking His disciples, saying, "Who do men say that I, the Son of Man, am?"

> ¹⁴ And they said, "Some say John the Baptist, others Elijah, and others Jeremiah or one of the prophets."
> ¹⁵ He said to them, "And you—who do you say that I am?"
> ¹⁶ And Simon Peter answering said, "You are the Messiah, the Son of the living God."
> ¹⁷ And Jesus answering said to him, "Blessed are you, Simon Bar-Jonah, because flesh and blood did not reveal this to you, but My Father who is in the heavens."
>
> (Matt. 16:13-17 NYLT)

Christ could not be clearer that there is absolutely no room for boasting on Judgment Day that you were smart enough to figure this whole justification thing out on your own. There is no room for pride that you mustered up enough faith to believe the Gospel message. No, in this passage Jesus explicitly excludes boasting, telling His disciples that they only believed because His Father graciously enabled them to.

We see this in numerous other passages in Scripture:

- **2 Peter 1:2:** "To those who have obtained like precious faith with us by the righteousness of our God and Savior Jesus Christ."

- **Philippians 1:29:** "...to you it has been granted on behalf of Christ, not only to believe in Him, but also to suffer for His sake."

- **Acts 3:16:** "And His name, through faith in His name, has made this man strong, whom you see and know. Yes, *the faith which comes through Him* has given him this perfect soundness in the presence of you all" (emphasis added).

• **Ephesians 2:8-9:** "⁸ For by grace you have been saved through faith. And this is not of your doing; it is the gift of God, ⁹ not of works, lest anyone should boast" (ESV).

As Paul concludes in Romans 4:

> ²⁷ Where, then, is boasting? It is excluded. On what principle? On that of observing the law? No, but on that of faith. ²⁸ For we maintain that a man is justified by faith apart from observing the law.
>
> Rom. 4:27-28 (NIV84)

II.B.2. Repentance is a Gift. Turning now to repentance, we read in Scripture that God "commands all men everywhere to repent" (Acts 17:30). But then we are told by Peter that God the Father has exalted Christ "to His right hand to be a Prince and Savior, *to give repentance* to Israel and the forgiveness of sins" (Acts 5:31; emphasis added). Who gives repentance and forgiveness of sins? Christ. Repentance is impossible for man apart from the regenerating work of the Holy Spirit. God grants repentance; man does not produce it.

We see this confirmed later in Acts, where we read that, "God has also granted to the Gentiles repentance to life" (Acts 11:18). Once again—God grants repentance; man does not produce it. Finally, the Apostle Paul instructs Timothy to "in humility correct[] those who are in opposition [so that] God perhaps will grant them repentance so that they may know the truth" (2 Tim. 2:25). In other words, the point of church discipline, the point of correcting false teachers, is the hope that God will grant them repentance. Again, God grants repentance; man does not produce it.

From start to finish, therefore, conversion is the effective and decisive work of God and God alone.

II.C. That God be Glorified. All of salvation—our election, our calling, our repentance and faith, our justification, our adoption, our sanctification, and our glorification—is by God and for God and to God, to whom alone be the glory forever. As we saw in Ephesians 1, this is the entire point of our salvation—to magnify, make much of, exalt, and glorify God:

- **Verse 6:** God choose and predestined in order to elicit praise of the glory—or display—of His grace.
- **Verse 7:** We have been redeemed to glorify—or demonstrate—the riches of His grace.
- **Verse 12:** Those who first trusted in Christ are to the praise of His glory.
- **Verses 13-14:** And that those who later trust in Christ are also to the praise of His glory.

Here are a few verses from Isaiah that demonstrate this as well:

- **43:7:** "Everyone who is called by My name,
Even for My glory I have created him,
I have formed him, yea, I have made him." (NYLT; emphasis added)
- **44:23:** "Sing, O heavens, for Yahweh has made it!
Shout, O lower parts of earth,
Break forth, O mountains, with singing,
Forest, and every tree in it!
For Yahweh has redeemed Jacob,
And in Israel He beautifies Himself." (NYLT; emphasis added)

- **49:4:** "And He saith to me,
'You are My servant, O Israel,
In whom I beautify Myself." (NYLT; emphasis added).
- **60:2:** "For, behold!—the darkness covers the earth,
And thick darkness the peoples,
And on you Yahweh rises,
And His glory is seen on you." (NYLT; emphasis added)
- **61:1, 3:** "[1] 'The Spirit of Adonai Yahweh is on Me,
Because Yahweh anointed Me
To proclaim good news to the humble,
He sent Me to bandage the brokenhearted,
To proclaim liberty to captives,
And the opening of prison to those bound...
[3] ...*That He may be beautified.*'" (NYLT; emphasis added)

We see this confirmed in 1 Peter, chapter 2:

[9] And you are a choice offspring, a royal priesthood, a holy people group, a people acquired, t*hat you might fully herald the excellences of Him* who called you out of darkness into His marvelous light; [10] who were once not a people, and now are the people of God, who had not found mercy, and now have found mercy.

(1 Pet. 2:9-10 NYLT; emphasis added)

We are saved, verse 9 tells us, that we might "fully herald" the praises of Him who saved us. Paul reiterates this in Ephesians, chapter 2:

> 4 But God, being rich in mercy, because of His great agape with which He agaped us, 5 even being dead in the trespasses, did make us to live together with the Messiah, (by grace you are saved), 6 and raised us up together, and seated us together in the heavenlies in Messiah Jesus, 7 that He might show in the ages that are coming the surpassing riches of His grace in His kindness toward us in Messiah Jesus. 8 For by grace you have been saved through faith, and this not of yourselves —but the gift is of God 9 not of works, so that no one can boast.
>
> (Eph. 2:4-9 NYLT)

Verse 7 makes clear that God saved us that for all eternity we might glorify Him as He shows us ever greater and greater manifestations—or glories—of "the surpassing riches of His grace in His kindness toward us in Messiah Jesus." Finally, as we read earlier from Romans 9, God predestined "vessels of wrath prepared for destruction" (vs. 22) in order to make His wrath and power known (vs. 22), so that He might display just how rich and incomprehensible His glory is to "the vessels of mercy which He had prepared beforehand for glory" (vs. 23).

III. God's Glory = Our Joy. So far we have looked at what we mean by God's glory and how justification is all for God's glory. Now, the third and final question we must ask is, since God does everything for His glory and His glory alone, how is He not an egomaniac? Or, to put it another way, is His pursuit of His glory at odds with our happiness? Or, to put it yet final way, is He simply using us to stroke His ego?

For Scripture is clear that God only acts for the sake of His name, for the sake of His praise, for the sake of His glory, for His own sake (Is. 48:9-11; see also Ex. 14:4, 17-18; 1 Sam. 12:20, 22; 2 Kings 19:34, 20:6; Ps. 25:11, 106:7-8; Is. 43:6-7, 25, 49:3; Matt. 5:16; Jn. 7:18, 12:27-28, 13:31-32, 14:3, 16:14, 17:1; Rom. 3:25-26, 9:17, 15:7; Eph. 1:4-6, 12, 14; 1 Pet. 2:12). That is what we mean by God's righteousness. God's righteousness is His absolute, unwavering commitment to glorifying His holiness, to magnify His infinite value and worth, to display the beauties of His attributes and character.

But it may well be that some reading this are slightly annoyed, turned off, and maybe even a little bit disgusted at a God so jealous for His own glory that He sovereignly created and controls the entire universe to maximize the fame of His name. For instance, let's imagine that on my wedding anniversary I gave my wife a book of poetry. That wouldn't necessarily be that unusual, except that this book contains 150 poems I wrote extolling *my* virtues, character, and attributes for her to delight in. And I even entitled the book, "Here are all the ways that I love me so that you can love me more." She, and you, would naturally conclude that I was a narcissistic pig in desperate need of a reality check with a side helping of humble pie.

But that is exactly what God did. He wrote the Psalms —150 poems, most if not all originally set to music, extolling His virtues, character, and attributes for our delight. In fact, over and over again He commands us in Scripture to praise Him. The following are but a brief sampling of the hundreds of such commands in Scripture:

• **Psalm 9:11:** "Sing praises to Yahweh who inhabits Zion! Declare His acts among the peoples!" (NYLT)

NATHAN W. TUCKER

- **Psalm 95:1-2, 6:** "[1] Oh come, we sing to Jehovah! We shout to the Rock of our salvation! [2] We come before His face with thanksgiving! With psalms we shout to Him!...[6] Oh come, we bless Him, we bow down, and we prostrate ourselves before Yahweh our Maker!" (NYLT)
- **Psalm 98:4:** "Shout to Yahweh, all the earth; break forth and cry aloud and sing." (NYLT)
- **Psalm 150:**

[1] Praise Yah!

Praise God in His holy place;

Praise Him in the expanse of His strength!

[2] Praise Him for His mighty acts,;

Praise Him according to the abundance of
His greatness!

[3] Praise Him with blowing of trumpet,

Praise Him with lute and harp!

[4] Praise Him with timbrel and dance,

Praise Him with stringed instruments and
flute!

[5] Praise Him with cymbals of sounding,

Praise Him with cymbals of shouting.

[6] All that does breathe praise Yah! Praise
Yah! (NYLT)

- **Romans 15:11:** "...`Praise the LORD, all you ethnic groups; and laud Him, all you peoples!'" (NYLT (quoting Ps. 117:1)).
- **Hebrews 13:15:** "Through Him, then, we may offer up a sacrifice of praise always to God, that is, the fruit of lips, giving thanks to His name!" (NYLT)

How, then, is God not evil for being an egomaniac? A narcissistic pig? How is He not merely a vain deity worthy to be despised rather than worshipped?

The solution to our difficulty lies in the fact that Yahweh, be very definition of being God, must be the infinitely and supremely valuable object in the universe. Or, to put it another way, that by very definition of being God He must be the infinite and supreme source of all joy in the universe. The infinite and supreme source of all pleasure in the universe. The infinite and supreme source of all satisfaction and contentment in the universe. If He is not all these things, He is not God.

Therefore, God must be entirely, one-hundred percent for Himself if He is to be for us at all. For if God would ever turn away from Himself as the infinite, supreme, and ultimate source of all joy, He would cease to be God. Why? Because it would make Him less than God—an idolater who would profane His name by giving His glory to another (Is. 48:9-11; Ezek. 20:14). If God, even for just one trillisecond, ever took His eyes off of Himself to pursue joy in worshipping someone or something else, He would deny and blaspheme His infinite worth. He would be nothing less than unrighteous and evil.

And if He would ever stop pursuing with absolute, unwavering commitment the maximum glorifying—or displaying—of the beautify of His holiness for all creation to enjoy in worship, He would not be loving. Why? Because by doing so, He would be denying all of creation that which would give them the most delight—namely, the joy of worshipping and delighting in God. When you love someone, you want them to have the very best, and so with God it is no different. God wants to give us His very best—namely, Himself. Therefore, in order to love us, God has to first love Himself supremely. Since the glory—or display—of the manifold beauties of God's nature and attributes is the only source for our supreme delight and passion, God—in order to love us—must relentlessly pursue His own glory. In order to be love (1 Jn. 4:8, 16), He must magnify—or glorify—His holiness for our eternal happiness and contentment.

Concluding Implications:

In conclusion, we first saw that by the term *glory*, we refer to the display or magnification of the beauties of God's holiness (i.e., His innate, infinite, perfect, and supreme worth). Secondly, we saw that justification is for God's glory because all of it—the foreknowing, the predestining, the calling, the justifying, the adoption, the sanctification, and the glorifying—is of God. There is no room for boasting except in Christ and Christ alone (Gal. 6:14). Third and finally, we saw that God is not an egomaniac because, to be a loving God, He has to be for Himself in order to be for us.

Therefore, *Sola Deo Gloria* means that God's glory—the display of the beauties of His holiness—is to be gloried in. Boasted in. To find as completely satisfying. To delight in as one's supreme joy. It is to find one's complete satisfaction in Christ and Christ alone. The chief end of man is to glorify—or to make much of—God *by* enjoying Him forever.

God is entirely self-sufficient and self-sustaining without need or want; He is eternally and infinitely perfect (Ex. 3:14). Therefore, He did not need to create anything. He does not need our praises. However, God has eternally existed as a Triune God whose love and goodness overflowed into the act of creation. God created man in His own image (Gen. 1:26-27) so that they might be caught up into this eternal love and joy between the three-in-one Godhead (Ps. 16:11; Jn. 15:11, 16:24; 1 Jn. 1:4). The purpose for which God created the world, therefore, is to be glorified by the joy, delight, happiness, and contented satisfaction of a Bride—the Church—in the worship and praise of Him.

Every human heart echoes with Moses when he cries out to Yahweh, "show me Your glory!" (Gen. 33:18). The problem is, most people don't realize that. Most people are in denial of the emptiness of their heart, consciously or subconsciously seeking to fill their desperate desire for lasting joy and contentment in romance, sex, drugs, alcohol, financial security, possessions, family, work, etc. But as Augustine noted in one of the most profound sentences every penned, "Because You have made us for Yourself...our hearts our restless till they find their rest in Thee."

As I close, therefore, I urge you to test yourself to see if, in fact, you are living for the glory of God (2 Cor. 13:5) by answering the following questions:

First, do you crave after holiness? Is the desire of your heart to be conformed to the likeness and image of the God-man Jesus Christ? We were created by God in His image so that we would reflect His character and thereby bring glory to Him. That is, after all, what images do. Much like a picture of the ocean, or a sunset, or a waterfall seeks to accurately depict the original in all its glory and thereby elicit praise of the original, so we are to imitate Christ in all His glory and thereby elicit praise to Him. So do others see Christ in you and thereby glorify God (Matt. 5:16; 1 Pet. 2:12)?

Second, is the aim of your life to glorify God? Do you seek to glorify Him in all you say, do, or think? Do you yearn to magnify His value and worth in every aspect of your life? 1 Corinthians 10:31 commands us that, whether we eat or drink or whatever we do, we are to do it all to the glory of God. Do you, therefore, wake up every morning seeking to maximize God's glory in what you do? Do you seek to glorify God in your family, your friends, your work, and your leisure? Or, to put it another way, do you enjoy other things not merely for their own pleasure and value, but to glorify God by His good gifts?

Third, is the desire of your heart to glorify God for who He is, and not for what He has or will do? In other words, do you merely praise God for His salvation, or also for His innate beauty? Do you find yourself praising God for what you hope He will do for you in the future, or also for His infinite holiness? Or, to put it another way, do you delight in God Himself or merely in what He has done for you yesterday or what He may do for you tomorrow? In short, would heaven be hell if you were there but God wasn't? Is God your heaven, such that you count all else rubbish to know Him and be found in Him (Jn. 17:3; Phil. 3:7-8)?

Fourth and finally, are you willing, if God wills it, to endure suffering, pain, and hardship if thereby He would obtain more glory? In 2 Corinthians 12, the Apostle Paul writes of a thorn in the flesh that he pleaded with God on three separate occasions to remove (vs. 7-8). God's answer was, "My grace is sufficient for you, for My strength is made perfect in weakness" (2 Cor. 12:9). Paul's response sprung form a heart devoted to God's glory, for he writes that, "most gladly I will rather boast in my infirmities, that the power of Christ may rest upon me" (vs. 10). Are you likewise willing to endure infirmities, reproaches, needs, and persecution for Christ's sake (vs. 11) in order for God's grace to be magnified in your life?

In conclusion, may the continuous refrain of our hearts be, "Not unto us, O Yahweh, not unto us, but to Your name give glory, for Your steadfast love, and for Your truth!" (Ps. 115:1 NYLT). "Through Him, then, we may offer up a sacrifice of praise always to God, that is, the fruit of lips, giving thanks to His name!" (Heb. 13:15 NYLT).

COMING WINTER 2025!

WHAT IS SAVING FAITH?

AN EXPOSITION OF MAN'S MOST IMPORTANT QUESTION

OTHER BOOKS BY NATHAN TUCKER:

Julia's Christmas Carol

Letters From Cell No. 73

Constitutional Musings: An Anthology of Legal Columns

We the People: The Only Cure to Judicial Activism

www.ingramcontent.com/pod-product-compliance
Lightning Source LLC
LaVergne TN
LVHW052024080426
835513LV00018B/2138